Stewards of Excellence

La raison agit avec lenteur et avec tant de vues, sur tant de principes, lesquels il faut qu'ils soient toujours présens, qu'à toute heure elle s'assoupit ou s'égare, manque d'avoir tous ses principes présens. Le sentiment n'agit pas ainsi: il agit en un instant et toujours est prêt à agir. Il faut donc mettre notre foi dans le sentiment; autrement elle sera toujours vacillante.

Pascal: *Pensées*

Stewards of Excellence

STUDIES IN MODERN ENGLISH AND AMERICAN POETS

BY

A. Alvarez

GORDIAN PRESS
NEW YORK
1971

Originally Published 1958
Reprinted 1971

Library of Congress Catalog Card Number — 70-159035
ISBN 87752-152-2

ACKNOWLEDGEMENTS

The author and publisher wish to thank the publishers indicated for permission to quote the following copyright material:

AUDEN, W. H.
"Consider" (copyright 1934 by The Modern Library, Inc.), "The Witnesses" (copyright 1945 by W. H. Auden). Excerpts from "Lay Your Sleeping Head My Love," "Voltaire at Ferney," (copyright 1940 by W. H. Auden); "Herman Melville," "My Second Thoughts Condemn" (copyright 1945 by W. H. Auden). Reprinted from *Collected Poetry of W. H. Auden* by permission of Random House, Inc.

CRANE, HART
Excerpts from "The Bridge: Poem;" "The Bridge: The Dance;" "The Bridge: The Tunnel;" "In Shadow;" "Voyages, II;" "At Melville's Tomb;" "Stark Major;" "For the Marriage of Faustus and Helen, III;" "Recitative." From *The Collected Poems of Hart Crane* by Hart Crane. By permission of Liveright Publishers, New York, copyright 1933 Liveright, Inc.

EBERHART, RICHARD
"The Fury of Aerial Bombardment" and excerpts from "Where Are Those High and Haunting Lines" from *Burr Oaks* by Richard Eberhart. (1947) Reprinted by permission of Oxford University Press, Inc.

ELIOT, T. S.
Excerpts from "Mr. Eliot's Sunday Morning Service," "Whispers of Immortality," "The Waste Land," and "Ash Wednesday," (*Collected Poems 1909–1935* by T. S. Eliot, copyright 1936 Harcourt Brace & Company, Inc.); "East Coker," "Little Gidding," "The Dry Salvages," "Portrait of A Lady," and "Burnt Norton," (*Four Quartets* by T. S. Eliot, copyright 1943 T. S. Eliot); *Murder in the Cathedral*, copyright 1935 Harcourt Brace & Company, Inc. Reprinted by permission of Harcourt Brace & Company, Inc.

EMPSON, WILLIAM
"Note on Local Flora," "To an Old Lady," "Missing Dates," and excerpts from "Success," "This Last Pain," and "The Teasers"from *Collected Poems of William Empson*, copyright 1935, 1940, 1949 by William Empson. Reprinted by permission of Harcourt Brace and Company, Inc.

FROST, ROBERT
"Lodged" and excerpts from "On the Need of Being Versed in Country Things," "Storm Fear," "Provide, Provide," "The Sound of Trees," "Black Cottage," "Never Again Would Birds' Song Be the Same." From *Complete Poems of Robert Frost*. Copyright 1930, 1949 by Henry Holt and Company, Inc. Copyright 1936 by Robert Frost. By permission of the publishers.

LAWRENCE, D. H.
"End of Another Home Holiday," "Red Geranium and Godley Mignonette," and miscellaneous excerpts from *Collected Poems, Last Poems*. Excerpt from *Kangaroo*. Reprinted by permission of The Viking Press, Inc.

5

ACKNOWLEDGEMENTS

LOWELL, ROBERT
Excerpts from "Quaker Graveyard in Nantucket" (*Lord Weary's Castle* by Robert Lowell, copyright 1944, 1946 by Robert Lowell). Used by permission of Harcourt Brace & Company, Inc.

POUND, EZRA
"A Girl" and excerpts from "Personae, 1908, '09, '10," "Homage to Sextus Propertius," "Hugh Selwyn Mauberley," and "The Social Order, II," from *Personae*, copyright 1926, 1954 by Ezra Pound. Excerpts from the cantos are from *The Cantos of Ezra Pound*, copyright 1934, 1937, 1940, 1948 by Ezra Pound. Reprinted by permission of New Directions.

RANSOM, JOHN CROWE
Excerpt from "Winter Remembered" reprinted from *Selected Poems* by permission of Alfred A. Knopf, Inc.

ROETHKE, THEODORE
"Cuttings" from *The Lost Son and Other Poems* by Theodore Roethke, copyright 1948 by Theodore Roethke. Excerpt from "I Need, I Need" (*Praise to the End* by Theodore Roethke, copyright 1951 by Theodore Roethke). Reprinted by permission of Doubleday & Co., Inc.

ROSENBERG, ISAAC
Excerpts from *Collected Poems* used by permission of Schocken Books, Inc.

STEVENS, WALLACE
Excerpts from "The Man with the Blue Guitar;" "An Ordinary Evening in New Haven, V;" "Metaphor as Degeneration;" "Notes Toward a Supreme Fiction, I;" "The Bird with the Coppery, Keen Claws," "Le Monocle de Mon Oncle, VI;" and "The Emperor of Ice-Cream;" from the *Collected Poems of Wallace Stevens* are reprinted by permission of Alfred A. Knopf, Inc.

YEATS, W. B.
"Sailing to Byzantium," "Memory," "Three Movements," "Politics," "A Deep-Sworn Vow," and excerpts from "Coole Park and Ballylee," "The Circus Animals' Desertion," and "A Song," reprinted from *The Collected Poems of William Butler Yeats* by permission of The Macmillan Company

Chapters I, III and V appeared originally in the *Twentieth Century;* Chapter II in *Essays in Criticism* and parts of the last chapter in *The Listener* and *The Times Literary Supplement.*

CONTENTS

PREFACE

THIS book is not intended to be a general guide to modern poetry. Yet neither is it a collection of wholly separate essays. With one exception, all the chapters were written within about fifteen months, and all, in their different ways, centre on two questions: first, since twentieth-century poetry has depended so much on the combination of English and American influences, what are some of the essential differences between the two traditions? Second, why have the great creative possibilities of modern poetry come, in fact, to so little?

The answers I suggest are, in the very broadest terms, that "modernism"—in inverted commas—has been predominantly an American concern, a matter of creating, almost from scratch, their own poetic tradition. It has affected English poetry peculiarly little. Instead, the most significant and powerful British geniuses, Lawrence and Yeats, were merely extending into modern terms what has always been there in the most vital of our tradition. To illustrate this I have, on a number of occasions, invoked the example of John Donne.

Such conclusions as there are have emerged, in a rather shadowy way, from detailed studies of individual poets. I have thought it better to leave the chapters as they are rather than to use my hindsight to force them into what would have been, I imagine, a spurious, though neater, pattern.

I would like to thank the Rockefeller Foundation for a most generous grant which enabled me to write the larger part of this book.

A. ALVAREZ, 1957

ELIOT AND YEATS

Orthodoxy and Tradition

*I hold—in summing up—that a tradition is rather a way of
feeling and acting which characterizes a group throughout
generations; and that it must largely be, or that many
elements in it must be, unconscious; whereas the maintenance
of orthodoxy is a matter which calls for the exercise of all
our conscious intelligence. The two will therefore considerably
complement each other*

T. S. ELIOT, "After Strange Gods"

*Our studies were useless or misdirected, especially our studies
in English Literature: the authors we were forced to read,
and Shakespeare most of all, were unpleasant to our palate.*

MALCOLM COWLEY, "Exile's Return"

I

My remarks will, for the most part, be general.
Eliot and Yeats are our founding fathers; on
them our inheritance depends. It is the nature
of that inheritance that is my subject. There is no longer
any need for patient elucidation of the texts. Commentaries on both poets are legion; there is probably not a
single long poem of Eliot's, and very few short ones,
which has not, somewhere or other, been put under the
microscope. What is now at stake is not Eliot's references and intellectual prowess nor Yeats's supernatural
machinery; it is what is left when these are taken for
granted, when the poets are read without a sense of
shock or indignation or even glee; when, that is, they

are read less as leaders under whose banners, or against whom we must fight, but as poets in literature, spokesmen of a plight more universal, however less absorbing, than our own immediate one. For the years of *l'entre deux guerres* are receding; Yeats is dead, Eliot has turned to the West End stage. The achievement of both is now something apart from their modernity.

The experimental trappings of modernism are a minor issue in English verse. It is largely an American importation and an American need. The American novel is already secure in its great masters: Hawthorne, Melville, Mark Twain and Henry James. But at the turn of the century the poetry had still very little to go on; Poe, Whitman and Emily Dickinson gave hints, showed possibilities; but they settled nothing. They lacked the power and the creative autonomy of great artists. Hence the constant preoccupation with technique—which has ridden Eliot and Pound as much as Amy Lowell and Cummings—and the hosts of good minor writers who seem sincerely and consistently to be doing their best to keep up the competence of versewriting. This absolute need to forge a new poetic language does not exist in England; the poets of the tradition are already there as a sort of framework for originality. Indeed, perhaps the incompetence of much of the writing of the 'thirties comes from a deliberate refusal to bother with problems which had already been thrashed out again and again; the requirements of a political attitude were more demanding. One generalization at least seems to hold good: in England the experiments of modern poetry mattered less than what went with them—the wakening of the active poetic intelligence after the poeticizing 'nineties. This toughness was, of course, largely Pound's doing, with his insistence on the difficulty of making verse and his reverence for the range and depth of the whole tradition of European civilization. Perhaps it needed someone outside the tradition to appreciate it as clearly as he did. Eliot took up what Pound had implied: intelligence and cosmopolitan sophistication. But this clear morning light of intelligence is also in the poetry of D. H. Lawrence, who had almost no part in transatlantic modernism, and in a lesser way—lesser because it was never fully matured—it is in the poetry of Rosenberg and Owen, who were dead before it had taken hold.

Eliot's intelligence and his cosmopolitan sophistication go together, yet are not one. They are like Yeats's intelligence and his incurable penchant for blarney; they make for the peculiar strength and wholeness when it comes. In Eliot, they have also helped to bring about his strangely divided influence. His cosmopolitanism let in a certain transient smartness and recourse to allusion; it has since fostered in the United States a cult of irony which has been smoothed into a pedagogical device; it has given that newness to some of Eliot's language because, as he has repeatedly explained, he learnt more from French, a particularly dandified French, than from English. Yet his cosmopolitanism was not the same as Pound's continentalism. The more Eliot derived from French practice, the more thoroughly he justified himself by reference to the English tradition. I suggest in the next chapter that the qualities Pound discovered in Laforgue and Corbière, Eliot praised in the Metaphysicals. Subsequent fashionable criticism, which has put all the stress on the technicalities of the conceit and has passed over Donne's colloquial intimacy and relative freedom from poetical device, shows in what direction Eliot was travelling when, for a little, he went hand in hand with Donne. He used him a great deal for his own purposes and was influenced by him very little. His poems in quatrains, for example, are all very close in style and tone; the same movement and the same elegance support both:

> In the beginning was the Word.
> Superfetation of τὸ ἕν,
> And at the mensual turn of time
> Produced enervate Origen.

and

> Donne, I suppose, was such another
> Who found no substitute for sense,
> To seize and clutch and penetrate;
> Expert beyond experience, . .

Yet the first has all the polish of Gautier and all the tricks of Laforgue, while the second has exactly the cadence of Donne's "The Extasie":

> So must pure lovers soules descend
> T'affections, and to faculties,
> Which sense may reach and apprehend,
> Else a great Prince in prison lies.

As they appear in Eliot's verse, what Donne and Gautier and Laforgue have in common, and what Eliot shares with all three, is little in essential tone and everything in certain technical qualities Eliot wished to emphasize. This is very different from those moments when Yeats writes like Donne:

Another emblem there! That stormy white
But seems a concentration of the sky;
And, like the soul, it sails into the sight
And in the morning's gone, no man knows why;
And is so lovely that it sets to right
What knowledge or its lack had set awry,
So arrogantly pure, a child might think
It can be murdered with a spot of ink.

I don't believe that Yeats had Donne at all in mind when he wrote this. He had read the Metaphysicals, but he never seems to have imitated them deliberately. Yet phrases like "That stormy white But seems a concentration of the sky" and "So arrogantly pure, a child might think It can be murdered with a spot of ink" are like nothing in English poetry so much as, say:

wee understood
Her by her sight; her pure, and eloquent blood
Spoke in her cheekes, and so distinctly wrought,
That one might almost say, her body thought.

They are alike in ease and vividness and unexpectedness of imagination; in that colloquial hesitation before the final triumphant pounce on the exact phrase to round the matter off. Eliot, on the other hand, approaches Donne, as he approaches all his other models, with an enquiring strictness, a sort of critical wariness, rather tight-lipped. He uses tradition, Yeats is in it.

All this is to distinguish between the different kinds of poetry, not to praise Yeats at the expense of Eliot. For Eliot's deliberateness is founded on something not at all deliberate: an infallible taste in poetry. No other critic has quoted so consistently without error. Few others have made their quotations seem so relevant to their time. Our interests and standards in literature are Eliot's creation. And of course this is something more profound than the enthusiasm aroused by a few well-timed articles. His critical pronouncements were made valid by his poetry. So he did more than change the standards of critical judgment; he altered the whole mode of expression in order to make room for his originality.

The process was founded on personal taste and urgent personal needs—the absolute necessity to make of various hints from various parts of literature his own personal style. Eliot's style has remained entirely to himself; imitations apart, it seems in fact to have had very little *direct* influence. But he has improved the technical equipment of poetry out of all recognition, and the sources, or excuses, of his innovations have become common property. Good verse since Eliot is the most consciously literary since the time of Gray and Collins. There is an extraordinary technical knowingness about it. To keep only to the source I have already discussed: when, before Eliot, a poet went to Donne, he went for a particularly personal idiom; Rosenberg, for example:

> And then, when Love's power hath increased so
> That we must burst or grow to give it room,
> And we can no more cheat our God with gloom,
> We'll cheat Him with our joy.
> For say! what can God do
> To us, to Love, whom we have grown into?
> Love! the poured rays of God's Eternity!
> We are grown God—and shall His self-hate be?

The masculine, independent tone of this, bolstered by casuistry, is Donne's (it sounds like "The Canonization"), but the language is that of the 1910s: the second of the three stanzas (I have quoted the last)

begins: "For all Love's heady valour and loved pain/
Towers in our sinews . . ." After Eliot, however,
something quite different happens:

> Dear love, these fingers that had known your touch,
> And tied our separate forces first together,
> Were ten poor idiot fingers not worth much,
> Ten frozen parsnips hanging in the weather.

The feeling of this has nothing to do with Donne; it is
far nearer Arnold's "Ah love, let us be true to one
another. . . ." But the language leans heavily on Donne;
indeed, the ironic tenderness relies a little on the fact
that the reader will pick up the allusion:

> And like a bunch of ragged carrets stand
> The short swolne fingers of thy gouty hand.[1]

What it amounts to is that Eliot's influence has created
a common literary background of the seventeenth
century, Dante, and certain French poets; it is a common ground not merely for allusions but for the
techniques a poet might be expected to use. The change
in the equipment of poetry is far more important than
any fashions *The Waste Land* set for, say, anthropology.

The influence of Eliot's poetry itself seems then to
have been critical more than creative. He has exerted
considerable corrective force on the art of poetry, but
has, in his own verse, directly fertilized little. This has
much to do with the extraordinary degree of finish on all
his work, from *Prufrock* onwards. He has moved from
perfect form to perfect form and, quite simply, left no

---

[1] I should, as a matter of conscience, point out that John Crowe
Ransom has told me that he had not read Donne's poem when he wrote
this. I apologize, then, for imputing to him poetic motives not his own.
But that a poet should have found himself independently inventing one of
Donne's conceits does, I think, show that their style and technique—their
'feel', that is—was extraordinarily widely known at the time.

room to do it better. Drama aside, only in the single poem published since the *Four Quartets*, the *Ariel* poem of 1954, has there been a failure of means; usually if you resist Eliot you do so despite the poetry. There is a massive purposiveness in his poetic progress which is almost Miltonic; a control and certainty in the writing that are as though a counter-weight to the usual themes of hesitation and denial. Except for the very early poems, modelled on Laforgue, Eliot has never been influenced by a writer. He digests him. Echoes, quotations appear, incorporated into a body of verse which is wholly Eliot's. The more he has written, the more thorough has this assimilation become. In *The Waste Land* and before it, the allusions were essential to the poetic effect; they were a sort of shorthand, providing, with the least fuss, a context for the poet's emotions and standards for his judgments. But as Eliot moved away from a general predicament—the disgust and despair which seem to have been the common tone of the 'twenties—and as he approached a particular solution in the Church, the poetry became less allusive. *Ash Wednesday* and the *Four Quartets* are full of other people's phrases, but the exact sources are no longer so important. They help most to the detached formality of the verse, and are present as though as texts for meditation or as authorities to save the poet the labour of proof. But the force of the poems is in their personal precision, in their controlled examination of motives.

It is for this reason that I repeated the commonplace about the importance of Eliot's criticism in substantiating the hints of his poetry. Both rely on a complete control of his subject. His criticism works by its suggestions, all moving towards one end, not by any knock-you-down logic. And his poetry has all the advantages of a highly critical habit of mind: there is a coolness in the midst of involvement; he uses texts exactly for his own purposes; he is not carried away. Hence the completeness and inviolability of the poems. What he does in them can be taken no further. The writers who tried to follow in Eliot's steps found themselves learning instead from his sources.

Eliot's most widespread influence, however, has not come from his critical tips, nor from his technical skill, but from what is implied in the word "control", his intelligence. It is of the same order as that of Donne or Milton. It gives the impression that anything he turned his attention to he would perform with equal distinction. In University jargon, he has a "fine mind"; and the jargon is to the point, because like Donne and Milton and Coleridge, and unlike Shakespeare, Wordsworth, Lawrence and Yeats, the strength of Eliot's intelligence lies in its training; it is the product of a perfectly orthodox academic education. Writing of his criticism, John Crowe Ransom remarked:

> It must look strange, except that we are far too used to the dullness of the official custodians of literature, that a critical achievement like Eliot's should be a phenomenon so rare, and seem so fabulous when it comes. The learning behind it is perfectly regular, and based generally on the academic sources of learning. The Universities should have produced scores of Eliot's, so far as his kind of intelligence is concerned, though one might wish to make reservations about its quickness, or its depth, which would probably be superior in any age.

The gifts are exceptional, the training regular. Perhaps

this is what has given him his extraordinary affection for all forms of orthodoxy (classicist, royalist, Anglo-Catholic); I am sure that it has, from the beginning, added to the power of his influence. The type of intelligence was recognizable; it was a token of intelligibility where, on a preliminary reading, none was immediately to be found. That is why Eliot became a culture hero with the intellectuals and Pound did not, for all that they insisted on much the same reading and on the same difficult techniques. Certainly, Eliot's work seemed to have a greater emotional concentration, the fragments were fused at a greater pressure; whereas often in Pound's verse the learning seemed to disperse rather than concentrate the effect. But in Eliot there were also obvious marks of a very powerful mind at work. What he wrote was obscure, original, personal; the form, as often as not, was startling, the development hard to follow. And yet it did develop; in all the difficulty it gave the impression of great discipline and control. Finally, with practice, the obscurity was seen to be a matter of the economy and delicacy with which the argument was pushed forward; and so he was read with a sort of pleasurable awe. In "Gerontion", for example, it was not the Shakespearian idioms ("That the giving famishes the craving"), nor the echoes of Middleton that soothed the reader; but the subtlety and command of the intelligence which had gone to make the meditation on history, forced him to take with equal seriousness what at first seemed arbitrary fragments—the names, the apparently unrelated actions.

I believe that a great deal of the gratitude owed to Eliot is not primarily for his originality, nor for his professional skill and deliberation, nor even for the way in which he expressed the mood of his time—all these are matters for admiration, even reverence; but the gratitude is for the dignity he gave back to poetry simply by writing in the full strength of his intelligence, and then by conjuring up a whole tradition of poetry to show that, of course, he was right. By the weight of this intelligence, its range and control, and by the effort it demanded of the reader in return, Eliot altered the whole landscape of poetry. "The only method", he once wrote, "is to be very intelligent." In the face of Eliot's work, Housman's *The Name and Nature of Poetry* seems like the last cavalry charge in modern warfare.

When I speak of Eliot's intelligence I am referring to something which is a long way from intellectualizing. That would have handed poetry over to the Universities and ended it in pedantry. Nor do I mean the cleverness of some of his earlier, rather Gallic compositions; though Eliot never struts in his elegant sophistication, he has walked, at times, very delicately. His intelligence is a matter of how much is brought to bear on the subject; it is, to use his own criteria, an immediate and whole fullness of feeling and thought. Other disciplines are relevant but subservient to the poetry; he has a sort of "I could an I would" relationship to them. It is this which gives the control and assurance to his poetic intelligence; it is an ability to serve his own purposes whilst never being confined to any one narrow and inconvenient area. His poetry is a sort of Jehu: the other disciplines fall behind in its train.

II

With all this talk of discipline the poetry itself is possibly missed. My business up to this point has been to separate out some of the strands for inspection; for it is the details which are easily inspected and judged that would count most heavily for his contemporaries. The total impact is more muffled and dispersed. Yet the moving force behind it is discipline, for discipline is the stuff of orthodoxy (I refer back to the quotation that stands at the head of this essay), and orthodoxy is made, not born. The intelligence, orthodoxy and the absolute control over his medium are qualities which have helped Eliot to some of the most formally perfect verse in the English language. I insist on the word "formally". He has had hard things to say about mechanical regularity of form. He replaced it by a much stricter formality of rhythm and relevance. His verse is formal without being regularized. His formality is that of a man who has his subject, his responses and his interpretation of them, not merely alive but accounted for inside him. Even when he seems to be most in debt to other poetry, the idiom is still quite his own:

> But at my back from time to time I hear
> The sound of horns and motors, which shall bring
> Sweeney to Mrs. Porter in the spring.
> O the moon shone bright on Mrs. Porter
> And on her daughter
> They wash their feet in soda water
> *Et O ces voix d'enfants, chantant dans la coupole!*

Marvell, *John Peel*, *The Banks of the Wabash*, a French primer and Verlaine all begin to set up their own echoes, and are all caught and blended into Eliot's own theme. The reader begins to respond in one way, only to find himself peculiarly under Eliot's control. It is a control of intention, a formality of purpose.

In *After Strange Gods*, Eliot remarked:

> I should say that in one's prose reflections one may be legitimately occupied with ideals, whereas in the writing of verse one can deal only with actuality.

Beneath the paradoxical gleam, the aphorism has its own profundity; and it sheds a strong light on Eliot's practice, on the kind of actuality he deals with, as here:

At the first turning of the third stair
Was a slotted window bellied like the fig's fruit
And beyond the hawthorn blossom and a pasture scene
The broadbacked figure drest in blue and green
Enchanted the maytime with an antique flute.
Blown hair is sweet, brown hair over the mouth blown,
Lilac and brown hair;
Distraction, music of the flute, stops and steps of the mind
over the third stair,
Fading, fading; strength beyond hope and despair
Climbing the third stair.

or here:

. . . there is a time for building
And a time for living and for generation
And a time for the wind to break the loosened pane
And to shake the wainscot where the field-mouse trots
And to shake the tattered arras woven with a silent motto.

There is no question of the reader being distracted with superfluous ornament, or left fumbling for a symbol. The images, as Eliot uses them, are inevitable. Yet their relations with the outside, observed world are highly formal. When, for example, Hardy writes:

The waked birds preen and the seals flop lazily

the scene has its own being apart from the poet. "The fieldmouse trots" is brilliant and imaginative and right, but he is there for the poet's purposes; it is as though he existed at a distance. These hard, clear images of Eliot's are not, of course, illustrations of a thought; they are part of it. He said of Dante that his "is a visual imagination". Eliot's, I think, is a formal imagination. The particular hardness of his verse comes less from the mere fixing of the sensibility in images than from the ordered quality of those images themselves. There is no irritation between them and the passages of argument. He has, to use another phrase from the essay on Dante, a very strict "logic of sensibility".

The images, then, are not part of a brute symbolism, like that of the Elizabethan allegorists, and yet they are not directly part of the outside world, the world that goes on, Eliot or no. The images present an actuality which is always judged or regulated to himself. This is what I meant earlier by Eliot's critical habit of mind; I will return to it again shortly. For the moment, my business is with the nature of the actuality. There is in it almost never any sense of delight; nothing seems to take charge of the poet, despite himself. Even the moments of greatest intensity and release—the "blown hair" passage quoted above or the beautiful seascape in section VI of *Ash Wednesday*—gather strength from something that is beyond the moment. We have been there before. These "winks of eternity" or of love have appeared in two or three guises throughout the whole of his work. They gain meaning and poignancy by this. So they have something of the shorthand quality of the quotations in *The Waste Land*. But they are more a reference to the whole *œuvre* than to the moment itself. This may seem a pitiful misunderstanding of the business of poetry; but to repeat, I am trying to isolate Eliot's kind of poetry, not to criticize him for what he does not intend. The moments of greatest intensity have, as Eliot presents them, a certain obliqueness, an allusiveness, a controlling detachment. It is a poetry apart. In comparison, *The Winter's Tale*, for example, draws to its climax with full religious solemnity: Paulina cries "It is required you do awake your faith", and so on. Yet when the statue finally embraces Leontes, all he can manage is:

> O, she's warm!
> If this be magic, let it be an art
> Lawful as eating.

The difference between Leontes' sense of delighted recognition and Eliot's when he writes:

> From the wide window towards the granite shore
> The white sails still fly seaward, seaward flying
> Unbroken wings
>
> And the lost heart stiffens and rejoices
> In the lost lilac and the lost sea voices . . .

is everything that is implied in that phrase "O she's warm". Even in the most intense moments of feeling in Eliot's verse there is never any sense of immediate and living response *from another person*. Even with the "blown hair" and the "hyacinth girl", the intensity is something seen and commented on, as though one-sided: "I should have lost a gesture and a pose". The hero of *The Confidential Clerk* is someone who "doesn't need other people."

Yet clearly Eliot's way is by no means inturned or self-regarding as, say, is Hart Crane's. He has maintained those standards of impersonality he set himself from the first. The hesitancy he dramatized in *Prufrock* and the *Portrait of a Lady* have become, as a creative habit of maturity, a deliberate patience in amassing materials, a willingness to wait for that certainty when "once in every five or ten years", as he wrote of Pound, the material "accumulates to form a new whole and finds its appropriate expression". His subject is always "the past experience revived in the meaning". He is, in some ways, a meditative poet. But this does not mean a poet who deals in abstractions; Eliot's meditations are meditations on experience, in which the abstractions belong as much as the images; they are all part of his particular cast of mind, the meaning he gives to past experience. But Eliot is, I think, a relatively indifferent, or uninterested, observer of the phenomenal world—though in his earlier poems he was a sharp observer of manners. He is instead a supreme interpreter of meditated experience.

His direct affirmations are always summings-up of this type, concentrations for which all the rest of his verse appears as so many hints. What is, to my mind, one of his finest pieces of writing, section II of *Little Gidding* is precisely the crystallization of "the past experience revived in the meaning" with a terrible clarity. The voice has the unpartisan honesty of "the familiar compound ghost", a man beyond life, like Tiresias in *The Waste Land* and Dante's Vergil:

> 'Let me disclose the gifts reserved for age
>   To set a crown upon your lifetime's effort.
> First, the cold friction of expiring sense
> Without enchantment, offering no promise
>   But bitter tastelessness of shadow fruit
> As body and soul begin to fall asunder.
> Second, the conscious impotence of rage
>   At human folly, and the laceration
>   Of laughter at what ceases to amuse.
> And last, the rending pain of re-enactment
>   Of all you have done, and been; the shame
>   Of motives late revealed, and the awareness
> Of things ill done and done to others' harm
>   Which once you took for exercise of virtue.
>   Then fools' approval stings, and honour stains.
> From wrong to wrong the exasperated spirit
>   Proceeds, unless restored by that refining fire
>   Where you must move in measure, like a dancer.'

In the scheme of the poem this section is hardly intended to be final. It is a sort of warning signpost, pointing away from an impasse. But it has more direct power than anything else in the *Four Quartets*. For it seems a subject that Eliot has lived with; he knows it from the inside. It is *The Waste Land* refined, matured and judged with the confidence of standards. But despair and denial in *The Waste Land* were there because of lack of standards, because of the impossibility of finding any solution. Here, dignified as renunciation, they seem in the tissue of life itself. Of course, the positive solution Eliot offers is not one that can be known consistently, still less presented with much directness. He can only suggest and rely on the "logic of sensibility" to give direction and order to the hints. Yet, in my experience, this passage is one that stays most forcibly with you when the poem is done; much of the rest seems a series of subtle and beautiful hints at something that is just beyond your grasp. It is a sense of the desolation of life which remains. Against the insistence that life attains its meaning in death is the nagging worry that the poetry is dealing with certain states of spiritual refinement in which those two words are interchangeable. And this worry is something more basic than not knowing the states Eliot describes, nor yet believing his beliefs, nor assuming the orthodoxy from which his formality receives its strength. Again to quote the essay on Dante, which prepared the way for all Eliot's subsequent poetry:

> My point is that you cannot afford to *ignore* Dante's philosophical and theological beliefs, or to skip the passages which express them most clearly; but on the other hand you are not called upon to believe them yourself. It is wrong to think that there are parts of the *Divine Comedy* which are of interest only to Catholics or to mediaevalists. For there is a difference . . . between philosophical *belief* and poetic *assent* . . . In reading Dante you must enter the world of thirteenth-century Catholicism: which is not the world of modern Catholicism. . . . You are not called upon to believe what Dante believed, for your belief will not give you a groat's worth more of understanding and appreciation; but you are called upon more and more to understand it. If you can read poetry as poetry, you will "believe" in Dante's theology exactly as you believe in the physical reality of his journey; that is, you suspend both belief and disbelief.

28

There is no difficulty in giving poetic assent to Eliot's world, for it exists by virtue of the purity and control of his writing. But there is a difficulty in accepting the conclusion which is everywhere implied; and that is not the orthodoxy, but the rejection and denial which the orthodoxy honours. (And Eliot's poetry, unlike Dante's, deals more or less entirely, though not always at the same concentration, with those conclusions.)

The development of Eliot's verse, from *Prufrock* to *The Waste Land, Ash Wednesday* and the *Four Quartets*, is not from hesitation to rejection to preparation and arrival; it is of a steadily intensifying withdrawal and denial. The sureness of the *Four Quartets* is in the sureness of their renunciation. It is here that my remarks on the formality of Eliot's verse take their place. The triumphant achievement of the *Four Quartets* is in the peculiar wholeness and isolation of their poetic world, despite the fact that, compared with Dante's or Milton's worlds, Eliot uses only the bare, essential structure; he has created his world without any of the "worldly" props of narrative or figures. It is an inner meditative world that is publicly wedded to dogma through the offices of a controlled formal poetic language. The success is well-nigh perfect; you move from meditation to glowing image hardly aware of the remoteness, and still less of the conclusions to which it is all leading. For little is explicit, still less didactic. Eliot has always worked obliquely, by suggestion and by his penetrating personal rhythms. His power is in his sureness and mastery of subject and expression. And this sense of inviolable purpose seems to remove his verse from the ordinary realm of human interchange.

He has created a world of formal perfection. It lacks the dimension of human error.

It cannot, for example, stand up to the personal, speaking voice. Where Eliot himself steps forward without formality, he steps often into bathos:

You say I am repeating
Something I have said before. I shall say it again.
Shall I say it again? . . .

It seems, as one becomes older,
That the past has another pattern, and ceases to be a mere
   sequence—
Or even development: *the latter a partial fallacy*
Encouraged by superficial notions of evolution,
Which becomes, *in the popular mind*, a means of disowning
   the past.
The moments of happiness—not the sense of well-being,
Fruition, fulfilment, security or affection,
Or even a very good dinner, but the sudden illumination—. . .

(My italics)

Personal lightness of touch is not one of his gifts. It is these flashes of rather heavy condescension that bring home how much depends on maintaining the decorum and formality of his poetic occasions. But the unguarded moments are rare; Eliot hardly ever speaks without clearing his throat. When occasionally he falters, it is usually in the opposite way: the writing evaporates into words. This verbal element was present in his early work as a Jamesian self-consciousness:

That is at least one definite 'false note.'

And it has at times led him into an involvement with words almost scholastic in its intensity. Two examples will be enough; the moments are well known:

You know and do not know, what it is to act and suffer.
You know and do not know, that acting is suffering,
And suffering action. Neither does the actor suffer
Nor the patient act . . .

And the way up is the way down, the way forward is the way
    back . . .

The intention and the kind of problem invoked are
both clear enough. But the way in which it is stated has
been reduced to a gesture; there is a hollowness to the
subtlety. Usually a gesture is a weary insistence on
personal beliefs already well known to the reader.
Eliot's gestures, on the other hand, have almost nothing
in them of personal conviction and everything of verbal
contrivance. It is the formal world of his poetry emptied
of the personal intelligence which gave it life and
meaning. It is a sort of verbal vacuum, the intellectual
orthodoxy and discipline caricatured, or as though the
intellectual will continued when all other personal fullness failed.

Eliot, in short, has created an autonomous poetic
world of great power, freshness of expression, intelligence, delicacy, subtlety; but it is a segregated world—
equal but separate. Its remoteness is precisely in its
orthodoxy. This has nothing to do with the fact that it is
a Christian world in a predominantly irreligious society.
It is that orthodoxy is a product of discipline, discipline
of the emotions, of the intellect, of the will; finally, the
discipline of the creative powers into an absolute command of technique. If Eliot is in a tradition, it is, I
think, a tradition of what might be called Puritan art,
which is never, to use his own word, "unconscious"

when concentrating for action, but always vigilant, critical and aiming always at a sort of superhuman perfection.

III

Eliot lacks, I said, the dimension of human error. For this reason I have coupled him with Yeats. For Yeats's strength lies in the magnificent way in which he accepts fallibility. This has nothing to do with his silliness, which is something less fortunate. It is a question of flexibility of tone:

> That is no country for old men. The young
> In one another's arms, birds in the trees,
> —Those dying generations—at their song,
> The salmon-falls, the mackerel-crowded seas,
> Fish, flesh, or fowl, commend all summer long
> Whatever is begotten, born, and dies.
> Caught in that sensual music all neglect
> Monuments of unageing intellect.
>
> An aged man is but a paltry thing,
> A tattered coat upon a stick, unless
> Soul clap its hands and sing, and louder sing
> For every tatter in its mortal dress,
> Nor is there singing school but studying
> Monuments of its own magnificence;
> And therefore I have sailed the seas and come
> To the holy city of Byzantium.
>
> O sages standing in God's holy fire
> As in the gold mosaic of a wall,
> Come from the holy fire, perne in a gyre,
> And be the singing-masters of my soul.
> Consume my heart away; sick with desire
> And fastened to a dying animal

It knows not what it is; and gather me
Into the artifice of eternity.

Once out of nature I shall never take
My bodily form from any natural thing,
But such a form as Grecian goldsmiths make
Of hammered gold and gold enamelling
To keep a drowsy Emperor awake;
Or set upon a golden bough to sing
To lords and ladies of Byzantium
Of what is past, or passing, or to come.

The Tower was published in 1928, *Ash Wednesday* in 1930. It is hard to conceive of two major poets so close in time who could write so differently on the theme of renunciation. There is an obvious primary difference in sensibility: the difference between the static, observed quality of

Blown hair is sweet, brown hair over the mouth blown. . . .

and the swarming fertility of Yeats's opening stanza. Neither poem is more marshalled in its progress than the other, but they move in opposite directions; one is a poem about acceptance, the other of regret. The simple point to make about Yeats's poem is that the logic goes one way, the feeling another; the young come off very much better than the old; "Monuments of unageing intellect" lose their grandeur when they are followed so closely by "paltry". His heart must be "consumed away" because there is nothing better left for it; which is quite different from the approval with which Eliot has quoted

Poi s'ascose nel foco che gli affina.

33

But it is the last stanza which defines most clearly Yeats's attitude to "the artifice of eternity". The insistence and determination of the opening of this verse is flatly contradicted by what follows. For it ends where the first stanza began:

> . . . set upon a golden bough to sing
> To lords and ladies of Byzantium
> Of what is past, or passing, or to come.

is another way of saying

> The young
> In one another's arms, birds in the trees . . .
> Fish, flesh, or fowl, commend all summer long
> Whatever is begotten, born, and dies.

The whole poetic effort, the purgation which will gather him "out of nature" "into the artifice of eternity", is made solely that he may celebrate better the world of love and creation and fecundity that he has left behind. The power of the poem comes from this ambiguous attitude: the poet's ironic tenderness and pity for mortality considered against eternity, and for the vanity of his own strivings for impersonality set against the immediate beauty and warmth of the created world.

The difference between Yeats and Eliot is not then that between the simple and the complex; it is between different kinds of subtlety. You go to Eliot for the controlled, original, allusive subtlety of mind and feeling, for whatever is not obvious or easily stated; to Yeats for the central, living subtlety, the tension between rage and generosity, impotence and desire, between, often, an attitude and truthfulness.

ELIOT AND YEATS

What is lasting in Yeats is traditional but not orthodox. Yet before that can be reached a great deal of
Yeats's theoretical cant ought to be swept up. It is not
necessary to do it here. Like Eliot, Yeats felt he had to
have the support of beliefs. But he could find no acceptable dogma. So, aided by his wife and certain congenial
spirits, he constructed for himself a system of beliefs
out of astrology, neo-Platonism and spiritualism. R. P.
Blackmur has shown how valuable *A Vision* was in
directing his creative powers and giving conviction to
his imagery. The hocus-pocus was necessary for Yeats as
a person. It is not essential to the poetry. While Eliot's
Christian orthodoxy is part of the order and allusiveness
of his writing, Yeats merely needed the complication of
his fairies and theosophy in order to write of the great
common world of the passions. His delicacy is all in the
poetry, not at all in the beliefs. In the labours of
practical criticism, for example, John Wain recently
found that he had simply to disregard the clues Yeats
gave to "Among School Children". And in the poem I
have just quoted, "perne in a gyre" sends you to a good
dictionary, not to *A Vision*. Where the system gets the
better of him—in say, "Byzantium" or "All Souls'
Night"—the poetry loses strength. The machinery
rumbles more than it works; it is like the witches
without Macbeth. But at its best there is an extraordinary firmness about Yeats's poetic world: Helen
and modern Ireland, Platonism, folk-lore and politics
all have the same immediate conviction. For they are
judged by the same values and presented with the same
purity of language.

The values are traditional and when taken simply—

which the poetry does not do—ideal. But there is a clear break between the tradition of Yeats's mature poetry and the tradition of his literary world. The latter has its say in his *Autobiographies*. It is those more than anything else that set Yeats apart from our time. The shrewdness and intelligence are all there, but they have to fight against the style. In 1922 Yeats was still writing the prose equivalent of verse he had put behind him when he published *The Green Helmet* in 1910. There is the same cadence, the same sort of self-conscious, inverting emphasis about:

> So masterful indeed was that instinct that when the minstrel knew not who his poet was, he must needs make up a man.

as there is in

> He stood among a crowd at Drumahair;
> His heart hung all upon a silken dress . . .

Yet the prose was published the year after "Easter 1916", "The Second Coming" and "A Prayer for my Daughter". Moreover, in the *Autobiographies* he defines himself almost solely in terms of the Rhymers and certain Irish political causes. There is no mention of Ezra Pound, who, according to tradition, influenced him a great deal, and there are only a couple of passing references to Joyce. Yeats defines his growth in terms of causes which he shows he knew well to be lost. In his public personality, as he chose to present it, the intelligence, which is everywhere, goes with a deliberate harking back.

Yet it is quite deliberate. Abstracted, the values which give strength to his mature poetry are not of our time. The *Autobiographies* show that they were still very much alive for him. They can be seen in his tributes to Lady Gregory, his themes of the aristocratic tradition, the country-house, the patron and the settled hierarchical society. That is what he had been brought up to; the standards he applied were, for him, far from idealized. In the poetry they are far stronger than his fabricated "beliefs". Only in Ireland, or perhaps in that other feudal museum-piece, Poland before 1939, could a writer have been born to a code of this type. And yet, of course, they had been at the back of English poetry since its beginning. That is why, for all his Irishness, I insist on discussing Yeats in the English tradition.

If he had all this, why did he fabricate a system of beliefs? It is a question of how keenly he realized his allegiances and his debts. There seems to have been something in his nature that made him unable to feel the power of what he could assume without doubting. In this he is the opposite of Eliot. Yeats's dogmas and orthodoxies encouraged in him a sort of triviality. In his maturity, his spiritualism was a game he played: he shuffled his symbols around, he quoted Plato and Plotinus as authorities, with a supreme disregard of the authoritativeness of his poetry itself. So, in his early verse: the aristocratic tradition became a dim mythology, nobility a rather dreary mountain-moving heroism and love a hopeless mist which enveloped everything. The Pre-Raphaelite mode in which he began and from which he fought free encouraged him in his taste for dreams. At the front of that decisive 1914 volume, *Responsibilities*, is a quotation (which I suspect he made up), "In dreams begin responsibilities". But the dreams give only a shadowy hint, the waking gives the substance. And waking from a dream is, literally, a disillusionment. That is the theme of his later work. We know roughly what those disillusionments were: with his love affair with Maud Gonne, with Irish politics, with the Irish audience for whom he was writing plays, and finally, under the influence of Pound, with the mode of verse he had practised. It all came together in this latter, where the influence was from an American. Yet the energetic craftsmanship Pound spoke up for was secondary. What mattered most was that he spoke for the cynical intelligence of the new world. That cynicism, despite all its lip-service, has nothing to do with the traditions Yeats was brought up in. The disillusionment of his maturity comes from the conflict which he saw the traditions of the old world losing to the new world of Pound and Eliot. And Eliot, for all his criticism of it, created in *The Waste Land* a monument to the destructive power of this new world; he brings in his orthodoxies, literary and religious, to shore up his ruins.

In Yeats's poetry the moving force is this clarity that comes too late: he knows his traditions and allegiances only when, for all practical purposes, they are finished, just as he marries late in life when his emotional sap has been dried up:

> We were the last romantics—chose for theme
> Traditional sanctity and loveliness;
> Whatever's written in what poets name
> The book of the people; whatever most can bless
> The mind of man or elevate a rhyme;
> But all is changed, that high horse riderless . . .

and

> I have not lost desire
> But the heart that I had;
> I thought 'twould burn my body
> Laid on the death-bed,
> *For who could have foretold*
> *That the heart grows old?*

The theme of Yeats's youth was nostalgia for what had never been; that of his maturity, something between regret and remorse for a way of life he valued too late.

A writer whose mind worked less through concrete images, or who felt the pity of what he had lost more indulgently and less strongly, would have lapsed, upon these discoveries, into wisdom. Talking of George Moore in *Dramatis Personae*, Yeats said: "his mind was argumentative, abstract, diagrammatic, mine sensuous, concrete, rhythmical". It is those qualities which distinguish him from, say, Robert Frost, who also dispenses a great deal of soured wisdom. In Yeats's poetry there is a continual tension between the bitterness of what he says and the strength and sweep with which he says it. Eliot has called him a poet of middle age. He seems to me to be the poet of old age in everything except his creative power. That went on growing.

> Those masterful images because complete
> Grew in pure mind, but out of what began?
> A mound of refuse or the sweepings of a street,
> Old kettles, old bottles, and a broken can,
> Old iron, old bones, old rags, that raving slut
> Who keeps the till. Now that my ladder's gone,
> I must lie down where all the ladders start,
> In the foul rag-and-bone shop of the heart.

It is a poem about his poetry and his life, about his early illusions and final desolation. The point I want to make is that the desolation is not destructive. "The Circus Animals' Desertion" was written when he was over 70. It has not the tenderness and delicacy of "Among School Children" (though that was not published until he was 63); but the bare power of the writing is even greater. The language is simple but without a touch of the commonplace; its concreteness preserves him from wise generalities; and it locates the scorn firmly where it belongs. In contrast, it gives to the poet, in the power and clarity of his writing, a certain magnificence.

The simplicity and concreteness of the writing, then, emerge as a kind of personal quality. John Wain pinned it down very well when he said, "Every word used is consonant with dignity and passion." The writing deals only with the concrete, the values behind it are valuable only as they become personal. It is in this that Yeats is at one with Shakespeare and Donne. They write what might be called a "poetry of action", a poetry, that is, in which everything is implicit; standards emerge and are judged only in terms of human action, as things happen. It is not pure dramatic poetry, being not a question of plot but of behaviour. The poet defines himself by his awareness and poise; his standards are as subtle and flexible as the interchange between people. The poetry has a stamp which is personal and direct. Clearly, this is very different from the more detached and critical awareness of Eliot's poetry. Yeats works relatively directly and spontaneously, Eliot analytically. He is always suggestive, turning the subject in front of you like a jewel, making facet after facet flash into life, until you realize how complex and yet how whole the thing is. There is no question of saying whose method is more effective. They are dealing with different worlds. And Yeats's world is one in which *method* has less absolute value.

Despite all the pride he took in his craftsmanship, Yeats's innovations are negligible; they have none of that dramatic importance of Eliot's. The most obviously "modern" apparatus he employs, his symbols, are effective almost in spite of the theory behind them. For he does not, in his real strength, use them as hold-alls of meaning, private and a little inscrutable. They merely do their work along with the rest of the poem. The symbolism in "Sailing to Byzantium" seems to me essentially the same as that in "Memory":

> One had a lovely face,
> And two or three had charm,
> But charm and face were in vain
> Because the mountain grass
> Cannot but keep the form
> Where the mountain hare has lain

or in "Three Movements":

> Shakespearean fish swam the sea, far away from land;
> Romantic fish swam in nets coming to the hand;
> What are all those fish that lie gasping on the strand?

This is not symbolism at all; it is powerful use of the most telling imagery to hand. Because the imagery is used, and works, there is no need to be explicit. In the longer poems the metaphors have to do more, but that is because the poet is dealing with more complex and varying material. It is a difference in profundity, not in the nature of the imagery. Yeats's business, like any poet's, was always to say what he meant in the most effective and immediate way, not to define anything. If you try to trace his idea of "Byzantium" through the letters, or look it up in *A Vision*, you limit and deaden the poetry, as illustrations inevitably spoil a novel.

Yeats's poetry then is modern with very little of the paraphernalia of modernism about it. It is modern because the tone of voice is that of the time. He may be magnificent, tender, ironical, or harsh, there is always a speaking voice that comes off the page. Nearly always, when he is most working himself up, that peculiarly unobstructed, intelligent honesty will break through—in the last lines of this, for example:

> A spot whereon the founders lived and died
> Seemed once more dear than life; ancestral trees,
> Or gardens rich in memory glorified
> Marriages, alliances and families,
> And every bride's ambition satisfied.
> Where fashion or mere fantasy decrees
> Man shifts about—all that great glory spent—
> Like some poor Arab tribesman and his tent.

With this honesty goes a willingness to face the disagreeable or shameful side of his feelings, and a pertinence in seeking out images and references which best suit his purposes, rather than, as in his earliest verse, those which soothe and flatter the reader.

None of these qualities, as Eliot has pointed out, is particularly modern. And clearly, Yeats is not modern in Eliot's way. He lacks not only the technical innovations, but he has too none of that rootless, well-read,

undercutting, cynical intelligence of Eliot's verse up
until 1925. With Yeats, the more he freed himself from
dead conventions and the more he was at one with his
time, the more traditional he became:

> How can I, that girl standing there,
> My attention fix
> On Roman or on Russian
> Or on Spanish politics?
> Yet here's a travelled man that knows
> What he talks about,
> And there's a politician
> That has read and thought,
> And maybe what they say is true
> Of war and war's alarms,
> But O that I were young again
> And held her in my arms!

It has all the trappings of the time—ironical references,
a mock grandeur stopped short by the indifferent,
colloquial half-rhymes—and yet it ends up sounding as
traditional as "O Western Wind". The simplicity is
perhaps deceptive: Yeats's skill is used in the opposite
way to Eliot's; not to create an autonomous poetic
world, but to break down the barriers of formality in
order to arrive at a naked personal strength.

The achievement is that these personal statements
stand alone. They are not, at their best, idiosyncratic.
The test is in the amount he had added to the common
stock of poetry. Reading through his *Collected Poems* for
this essay I found I knew phrase after phrase, though
they came in poems I had utterly forgotten; they had
become part of my literary awareness, like lines from
Shakespeare or Chaucer. Yeats has the gift of all major

poets that, though the large bulk of his writing may contain many indifferent poems, there is hardly one without something that sticks in your memory. His poetry bristles with lines which, once you have read them, seem completely inevitable; lines which, by their purity and economy, add a fresh dimension to the language. They give a new norm by which to judge poetic expression. It would be easy to fill several pages with examples of this; to take three simple ones, all rather similar:

> To flatter beauty's ignorant ear;
>
> A young girl in the indolence of her youth;
>
> Bodily decrepitude is wisdom; young
> We loved each other and were ignorant.

Like Eliot, Yeats had the ability to add to his earlier poems by going on to write others. All these three fragments have a similar theme; it is the attitude behind each that is different, and the language is so controlled that even within the limits of rather similar wording the variety of the responses is quite plain. And this is unlike Eliot's "hyacinth girl", where the language has more variety but the attitude is static. It is Yeats's emotional resources that seem endless; not because they are always so original; they aren't; but they are always right. Quotations from him strike home first because of their centrality: that is what the feelings are like; then there is their spare, muscular freshness of language. Yeats has the great central human view, a little like Tolstoy, though not so profound nor so wide-ranging. Behind this centrality is the weight of a

whole tradition which has concerned itself with much
the same themes.

When you quote Eliot, it is in a different and more
complicated way: the words take hold before they are
quite understood. There is a feeling that something profound and original is being said. There is, too, an assurance and economy in the diction; the poet obviously
knows exactly where he is going. But as often as not
you are forced along without any immediate understanding to guide you. Perhaps this in some way
accounts for the pervasiveness of his influence: the
renunciation and denial are less inevitable than the
way they are put. The words are part of you before
you have them quite sorted out. This is not to say that
Eliot is muddled or unclear. But what he has to say is
usually difficult and original. The striking originality
of the expression makes you adapt to him.

In language Yeats and Eliot are quite apart. Yeats
has his share of the unexpected:

> I offer to love's play
> My dark declivities

or

> To find once more,
> Being by Calvary's turbulence unsatisfied,
> The uncontrollable mystery on the bestial floor.

And he has his exoticisms:

> Neither catalpa tree nor scented lime;

But his norm is always the spoken language. Eliot's
vocabulary strikes me as that of a fundamentally better
educated man, or at least of a man who has derived a

45

great linguistic satisfaction from his reading. Compare, for example, high points from both:

> The loud lament of the disconsolate chimera

and

> But Love has pitched his mansion in
> The place of excrement.

In Yeats's lines there is not a word that is not in everyday speech. Whilst the three striking words in Eliot's line, "lament", "disconsolate" and "chimera", though they are all perfectly usual, are all chosen from the written language.

It is this use of prepared language which makes Eliot more orthodox than traditional. It is not a "poetic" language, not nearly as "poetic" as Yeats can be when he sets himself to it. But Eliot's is a language of discourse, never of talk. There is always an element of design in it, which goes with the earlier experimentation and with the formal perfection he has attained. Writing of Yeats, Eliot said: "The kind of poetry that I needed, to teach me the use of my own voice, did not exist in English at all; it was only to be found in French." At this time, of course, Yeats was still writing in a mode which Eliot saw to be creatively outworn. But the choice of modelling himself on a foreign language would not have been possible for Yeats. What he did eventually derive from the Symbolists were mere surface tricks. As an American, Eliot could make free with the whole of European poetry, for the American language is not bound to English. I think this quest for a language and form for American poetry has been ended by Eliot. He has laid down the elements of a new tradition, one in which French and Italian practice is as important as English. The disciplined, formal perfection of his poetry provides a sort of code of manners by which the rest can be measured; the orthodoxy lays out the boundaries for the kind of life it can contain. The question now is whether this autonomous poetic world is fertile enough for other American poetry. Yeats's poetry is the new flowering of a very old tree.

EZRA POUND

Craft and Morals

I

But it is Pound, more than Whitman, Emily
Dickinson, or even Eliot, who is the first really
American poet; the first, that is, who, despite all
the literary machinery of his verse, has nothing to do
with the tradition of English poetry. His Americanism,
of course, involves much that is beyond the scope of this
essay. In recent years he has, for instance, become its
victim: his obstinate insistence that he is free to hold
whatever political opinions he pleases has led to his ten-
year confinement in a mental hospital. And Pound's importance as a figure on the American scene does owe
something to the fact that he is, so far as I know, the
first major artist to be held as a political prisoner since
the Nazis took Alban Berg. I will have nothing to say
here of Pound as a person. This essay was drafted before
I met him; although I have altered a number of details
since then, the critical judgments on which it is based
remain unchanged.

American scholars are much given to tinkering with
Pound's machinery. The English Institute, for example
met in 1953 to discuss him in great seriousness and
detail; he is the sole subject of a solemn periodical,
The Pound Newsletter; and Mr John J. Espey has
recently come forward with a long investigation of
Mauberley, done in the manner and with much of the

thoroughness of Lowes's *The Road to Xanadu*. Although much of the work is admirable and, in Mr Espey's book, illuminating, although some of it is even necessary, Pound is in danger of being swallowed up by his researchers. Under it all the original poetic voice is easily lost.

In England, on the other hand, it has hardly been heard. Pound is accorded the weary applause due to a man who, whatever else he achieves, is important in literary history: he gave Eliot his start, and Joyce, and Wyndham Lewis; he helped Yeats find his colloquial strength; he is, as Mr Eliot has remarked, "the inventor of Chinese poetry for our time", and also that of Provence; his critical tips are still current; finally, by tightening up the language and making sensitive the rhythms of verse, Pound is literally the inventor of the accepted medium of modern poetry. Despite all this, he is very little read. Of the thousand-odd pages of his poetry, only *Mauberley*, *Propertius* and *The Seafarer* are common property; add a few lyrics and epigrams and some fragments of the *Cantos*, the rest goes virtually unopened. Perhaps this is inevitable in a poet of Pound's output: the sheer bulk of it tells against him; the reader can only select. But I think with Pound the selection has been done by a very few enthusiasts, the readers rarely hunt for themselves. In England the *Cantos* are probably as little read and even less theorized on than *Finnegan's Wake*. It is not merely the bulk of the writing that is forbidding, it is the unwieldy masses of oddly assorted learning with which Pound has stuffed it, and his cheery assurance that his readers will, with the least formality, get acquainted with the intimate details of his reading and associations. There is something of a Daisy Miller in the poet of parts of the *Cantos*.

There is too a kind of irritating awkwardness with the tradition, even when his writing and his influence bring him closest to it. Set against his immediate predecessors and against most of their Victorian forebears, Pound is artistically puritanical yet colloquial, serious, original, vigorous, straight. Those qualities in him and in Eliot have made the present poetic continuum wider and deeper than it was. It has made us aware of something which is, in fact, very different: the independence, naturalness and intimate off-hand intelligence of the seventeenth-century poets. But Pound seems to have come at those qualities indirectly and, to judge from his earliest volumes, almost despite himself. His pronouncements on English poetry are uncertain, sporadic and biassed. He has come forward with some extraordinary statements in his time. For instance, in 1927 he wrote of four classes of poets; the lowest was:

> The men who do more or less good work in the more or less good style of a period. Of these the delightful anthologies, the song books, and choice among them is a matter of taste, for you prefer Wyatt to Donne, Donne to Herrick, Drummond of Hawthornden to Browne, in response to some purely personal sympathy, these people add but some slight personal flavour, some minor variant of a mode, without affecting the main course of the story.

(How to Read)

My instincts tell me he doesn't know what he is talking about. Then I remember that this was published ten years after *Propertius*, seven after *Mauberley*; they are both testament enough that he knew very well. Putting aside trivial reasons for this aberration (at 41 he would hardly have felt the need to shock; but he *may* only have read these authors as they appear in the song-books), it seems that Pound, when he wants to, is capable of an extraordinary singlemindedness in his reading. He has a wonderful ear for verse and a firm conviction that the true art of singing had been lost in English poetry in effect since Chaucer ("Shakespeare as supreme lyric technician is indebted to the Italian song-books, but they are already EXOTIC", *ABC of Reading*). And so he set himself to revive our sensitivity to the music of words: his first translation of *Donna Mi Prega* has a "*Dedicace*—To Thomas Campion his ghost, and to the ghost of Henry Lawes, as prayer for the revival of music". He seems to have devoted himself so wholly to his task that he could read with all his critical attention not exactly on the sound of the thing but on something that needed more brain-work, the technique of the sound. Caring so much for this, he seems hardly to have bothered with the tones of meaning, or, as in his side-swipe at Donne, with originality which enlarged the whole range of experience possible in verse.

And yet he produced *Mauberley* which, Dr Leavis said, has "a subtlety of tone, a complexity of attitude, such as we associate with seventeenth century wit". Although he did so without, as it appears, any clear idea of the native English tradition, or of seventeenth-century poetry, he did not come to it unprepared. His real flair and insight was for the poetry of other languages. The sophisticated intelligence of *Mauberley*, its ironical use of learning and the deflating cliché, the

51

apparent colloquialisms where every word is, in fact, scrupulously weighed, derive not from, say, Marvell, but from Laforgue and Corbière. What Pound found in them, Eliot praised in the Metaphysicals. They went at it from different ends—one admiring the skill, the other the wholeness and honesty of the response—but they finished with the same standards of accomplishment. Mr Espey's book shows how much *Mauberley* derives from Gautier in its ideal of the chasteness of language, in its references and images. I feel he underestimates the pervading influence of Laforgue on the tone. But it hardly matters. The important point remains: Pound wrote one of his few major works that has been generally acclaimed, in which he comes closest to a vital and difficult English tradition, at the moment when he was modelling himself most closely on French poetry.

This, I think, is a general rule for Pound's work, not an exception: he is at his best when most actively putting the strengths of another language in English—which is something quite different from the moments when he tries to write English and fails. As an example, I would like to set an early translation of Propertius against a section from the *Homage* (Mr Kenner has used these two poems, but to make different points):

Here let thy clemency, Persephone, hold firm,
Do thou, Pluto, bring here no greater harshness.
So many thousand beauties are gone down to Avernus,
Ye might let one remain above with us.

With you is Iope, with you the white-gleaming Tyro,
With you is Europa and the shameless Pasiphae,

And all the fair from Troy and all the Achaia,
From the sundered realms, of Thebes and of aged Priamus;
And all the maidens of Rome, as many as they were,
They died and the greed of your flame consumes them.
                    (*Personae*, 1908, '09, '10)

Persephone and Dis, Dis, have mercy upon her,
There are quite enough women in hell,
                    quite enough beautiful women,
Iope, and Tyro, and Pasiphae, and the formal girls of Achaia,
And out of Troad, and from the Campania,
Death has his tooth in the lot,
                    Avernus lusts for the lot of them,
Beauty is not eternal, no man has perennial fortune,
Slow foot, or swift foot, death delays but for a season.
                    (*Homage to Sextus Propertius*, 1917)

In the early version Pound is out to translate the words,
no matter what; even at the expense of the English
itself. Archaisms jostle with coy periphrases ("Ye
might let one remain above with us"); lines are padded
with expressions that do not exist outside translators'
dialect ("as many as they were"); there are awkward
inversions. The later poem is not so much a translation
as variations on a theme by Propertius. Pound does in
English what the Latin poet had done in his own
language; he uses the resources of the language to its
full, creating new, individual rhythms which are not
those of Propertius, yet give a taste to the verse which
is not quite English. They are the outcome of his
critical reading of Propertius. By that I don't merely
mean that Pound discovered the irony in Propertius
and created from him yet another *persona*. It is something in a way more thorough-going. He is literally

53

writing Latin verse in English, using the same quality of language as he finds in Propertius—colloquial, resonant, or ironic—and using it in what is basically a Latin metre:

> There are quite enough women in hell,
> quite enough beautiful women . . .
> Death has his tooth in the lot,
> Avernus lusts for the lot of them . . .

These are both more or less regular elegiac pentameters —less regular only because they have been accommodated to the cadence of the English idiom. So much has Pound made the Latin verse his own that the foreign quantitative metre emphasizes the native speaking emphasis: for example, in the first line the caesura is used to administer the ironic shock of the unexpected word "hell". Certainly, *Propertius*, like *Mauberley*, is also an ironic survey of Pound's own time and place; in it the Roman becomes curiously modern:

> Annalists will continue to record Roman reputations,
> Celebrities from the Trans-Caucasus will belaud Roman celebrities
> And expound the distentions of Empire,
> But for something to read in normal circumstances?
> For a few pages brought down from the forked hill unsullied?
> I ask a wreath that will not crush my head.
> And there is no hurry about it;
> I shall have, doubtless, a boom after my funeral,
> Seeing that long standing increases all things
> regardless of quality.

It is this that gives him that resilience and intelligent sense of proportion which reminded Dr Leavis of the seventeenth-century poets; they too were soaked in classical literature. The difference is that Pound does not, as most modern poets might, get at the Latin through the seventeenth century. He seems to work directly through the foreign language. And this is the essence of his best writing. It owes its freshness and economy to this power of using words as if he had just coined them. His language has no literary incrustations. He is the only poet in the last three hundred years to write English as though he had never read Shakespeare. For with Shakespeare the English language crystallized out. The imaginative fullness, the power and flexibility of Shakespeare's verse has been the abiding fact for every subsequent major poet. His originality and strength is what is left to him after he has fought it out with Shakespeare. But Pound has had no part in that fight. When I suggested this to him, he replied that his literary ancestor was Dante. He has, in fact, struggled with translation and with the business of writing verse to foreign plans. Yet it has left him a language that is curiously his own, curiously undisturbed by the English tradition that preceded it. It is for this that I have called him the first really American poet.

His achievement depends directly on his ability as a translator, or, more accurately, on his growing intimacy with the poetry of other languages and the skill with which he adapted their techniques to English. Pound has two poems in *The Oxford Book of Victorian Verse*, and they sit there not at all uncomfortably. In the very beginning he, like Yeats, was not set apart from the members of the Rhymers' Club by any startling originality of mind or truth to feeling. But he was energetic and devoted; he was willing to give himself wholly to the sheer hard grind of discovering, reviving and putting into practice the art of using language to its fullest. What there was to hand at the turn of the century was useless; the language had grown loose and nerveless since it was never called on to perform more than the dullest and most habitual tasks. So again and again Pound went to other literatures. His gradual advance from the Browning-and-haze of *Personae*, 1908, '09, '10, to *Ripostes*, 1912, *Lustra*, 1915, and finally *Mauberley* in 1920 is the outcome of the continual effort and discipline of translation. His *Cavalcanti*, appeared in 1912, so did *The Seafarer*; *Cathay*, the paraphrases of Fenellosa's notes, came out in 1915; the *Noh Plays* in 1916; *Homage to Sextus Propertius* in 1917, and the *Arnaut Daniel Poems*, which in the accompanying technical essay he said he had been at work on for ten years, were printed in 1920. The translations, in fact, were the ground bass of his most productive period, which culminated in *Propertius, Mauberley* and the earliest *Cantos*.

The difference between the early and the later volumes is more than skill—although now the epigrams are interesting chiefly for what they led to; it took practice in

> Her two cats
> Go before her into Avernus;
> A sort of chloroformed suttee. . . .
> ("The Social Order, II", *Lustra*)

to achieve the speed and polish of *Mauberley*'s "Dowson found harlots cheaper than hotels". Often the early poems seem skilfully enough done, but the skill seems to dissipate itself into the air; he has so little to say. Translation presented more than the technical problem of finding the exact words; it provided Pound with ready-made occasions for writing, upon which his very real feeling for literature could come into play. At his best, other literature is always an *occasion* for Pound. Instead of translating word for word, he seems to get on the inside of a work and recreate it outwards. His translations seem to me more original and more personal than those poems in which he has only himself to rely on. In *Ripostes*, for example, is a piece which Mr. Eliot has praised in his Introduction to the *Selected Poems*. It is of arguable but rather typical merit:

A GIRL

The tree has entered my hands,
The sap has ascended my arms,
The tree has grown in my breast—
Downward,
The branches grow out of me, like arms.

Tree you are,
Moss you are,
You are violets with wind above them.
A child—*so* high—you are,
And all this is folly to the world.

"There, you see," says Mr Eliot, "the 'feeling' is original in the best sense, but the phrasing is not quite 'completed'; for the last line is one which I or half a dozen other men might have written. Yet it is not 'wrong', and I certainly could not improve upon it." I feel Mr Eliot is too modest and rather too involved in his inverted commas. I am not at all sure how original

57

the "feeling" is. The young girl as a tree, the stripling, is after all something of a cliché. What originality there is lies in the way Pound has elaborated it into a sort of late Victorian conceit. But whether the impulse is a flickering mood or whether it is ingenuity, he seems not to know what to do with it. Far from "completed", the last stanza has been faked: Wordsworth's "violet by a mossy stone" is half-hidden in it. It is literary in the bad, the tricksy-tricksy sense.

The same image and something of the same intention recur in *Mauberley*, but this time in the form of a quotation:

> "Daphne with her thighs in bark
> Stretches toward me her leafy hands,"—
> Subjectively. In the stuffed-satin drawing-room
> I await The Lady Valentine's commands,
>
> Knowing my coat has never been
> Of precisely the fashion
> To stimulate, in her,
> A durable passion;

Mr Espey has pointed out that these first two lines are from Gautier's *Le Château du Souvenir*:

> Daphné, les hanches dans l'écorce,
> Etend toujours ses doigts touffus;
> Mais aux bras du dieu qui la force
> Elle s'éteint, spectre confus.

The "feeling" for the Lady Valentine may perhaps be less "original" than in *A Girl*; it is certainly sharper and more alive. The attraction, the mood, is seen in the round: real but one-sided ("Subjectively") and a little grotesque (the shabby poet is a long way from "le dieu qui la force"). Yet at the same time the Lady in her "stuffed-satin drawing-room" falls far short of his ideal of pagan sensual grace. They are all judged, the poet and his mood, Lady Valentine and her circumstances, through the quotation. It voices the poet's feelings at the same time as it allows him to step outside and examine them in perspective. In *Mauberley* there is the mood and the play of mind upon it, where in the first poem there was only a play of words.

Pound on his own, in fact, is not particularly full. Pound working through other literature is. He needs the framework of translation. It keeps his intellect and imagination at full stretch by providing for all the technical business whilst he sustains his understanding of the poem and the poet. Within those limits he recreates the feeling for himself. As a poet he moves, thinks and feels with the greatest ease and strength in other men's clothes.

II

Pound's superb craftsman's intelligence seems then not quite geared to what he feels outside literature; as though his response to experience as he lived it were not inadequate, but of a different order to the technical subtlety at his command. For me, one of the main troubles with the *Cantos*[1] is not their obscurity but their remoteness. They refuse to fix themselves with any sort of inevitability. Again and again there are passages of great beauty, but they are remote, done for their own sakes; the poet himself seems hardly to exist. Even

[1] That is, *Cantos I-LXXIII*. I discuss the *Pisan Cantos* in the final section of this essay.

the finest cantos have this evasive, centreless quality.
A number of moments from literature, each recreated
in its own terms, are held together by a loose flow of
association and a tenuous theme which the reader
himself must supply. Number II, for example, culmin-
ates in a long translation-paraphrase of the third book
of Ovid's *Metamorphoses*:

> And where was gunwale, there now was vine-trunk,
> And tenthril where cordage had been,
> > grape-leaves on the rowlocks,
> Heavy vine on the oarshafts,
> And, out of nothing, a breathing,
> > hot breath on my ankles,
> Beasts like shadows in glass,
> > a furred tail upon nothingness.
> Lynx-purr, and heathery smell of beasts,
> > where tar smell had been,
> Sniff and pad-foot of beasts,
> > eye-glitter out of black air.
> The sky overshot, dry, with no tempest . . .

The whole passage, there are three pages of it, is an
extraordinary *tour de force*; the choice of clear, strange
details coupled with the chanting rhythm, again based
on the Latin metre, set the scene in a hard, dry, powerful
light. Yet it remains, most persuasively, an artistic
performance. The language is so impeccable that it will
not stretch itself to do a jot more than its immediate
job. When language is, to use Pound's definition of
great literature, "charged with meaning to the utmost
possible degree", it radiates out from its situation,
forcing the reader back into his own experience, not to
complete the verse, but to add to it, as a boulder gathers

mass with momentum. Pound's language stays on the page; its accuracy and economy guard the reader against going any further than the single poetic moment. Each passage seems isolated, self-contained, almost ornamental.

Yet they are strangely moving. For all their remoteness they have a powerful existence of their own, though it almost never touches earth. It is partly a matter of the clarity of the writing and the extraordinary accuracy of the detail. And partly the care that these entail; it seems to come from something deeper than the apparent disconnectedness suggests. Behind it is a sort of awe of the past and of its literature, a belief that these things have, in Pound's contemporary cultural waste land, an inherent value of their own. It is this passionate antiquarianism which invests the remote with a queer, moving force, and yet, with an equal passion, preserves its remoteness. For all their scope, the *Cantos* are very specialized poetry.

Pound has always technique at his command, even when he is using it to be aggressively unpoetic, busily transcribing historical documents, or even, at moments, pastiching Ring Lardner. His style is as adequate to his whims as to his sober purposes. This is why the *Cantos* are never really difficult: he says what he wants very skilfully, and he never has anything very difficult to say. *Ash Wednesday* is obscure because it demands so much of the reader; preconceptions and obfuscations have to be stripped away in order to follow the delicate unfeigned shifts of feeling and argument. In the *Cantos* I find myself often at a loss for the reference; I want to know who the characters are, what books he is referring to, quoting from, paraphrasing. Their obscurity, in fact, is largely in the keeping of a competent editor.

But not quite. The other difficulty is more insoluble: weighing against his artistic concentration is Pound's inveterate garrulousness. The *Cantos* have too much in them. Keeping his own purposes so much in the background and excited by the past and the remote, it is enough that one thing should lead to another. "The secret of his form is this:" said Allen Tate, "conversation. *The Cantos* are talk, talk, talk . . . The length of breath, the span of conversational energy, is the length of a Canto. The conversationalist pauses; there is just enough unfinished business left hanging in the air to give him a new start; so that the transitions between *The Cantos* are natural and easy." The transitions within the *Cantos*, however, are far from easy. They seem to depend on nothing more than what Pound happens to think of next. So, for all the impersonality, the poet demands of the reader a considerable trust, as he leads him blindfold through his complicated maze of literary facts and figures.

Commentators on the *Cantos* warn continually against reading for the plot. They substitute a host of technical theories; they quote Pound's hint to Yeats on the permutation of themes and figures. But Yeats was notoriously gullible; he seems to have been overcome by the grandness of the gesture, "scribbled on the back of an envelope", for it is meagrely justified in the *Cantos* as they stand. The general theme of the work is clear enough: the quest for civilization and the descent into corruption of a number of societies and times, classical, Renaissance, Chinese, American, contemporary. But that is so large that it brings the reader no nearer than to be told that in *Finnegan's Wake* a man is born, lives, copulates, dies. Both works, by their careful surface detail, seem to offer something more complicated and exact.

We are told to read not for the plot but between the lines—Hugh Kenner, in *The Poetry of Ezra Pound*, has suggested that Pound has erected the scaffolding with great care and deliberately left out the bricks. Pound himself says that the *Cantos* are built up like a fugue: themes and phrases recur; nearly all the women, for example, turn out in time to be Circe. By attending patiently to the details the drift of the thing will eventually appear. But theories, technical details, even artistic accomplishment run into the ground too soon in a long poem. The singleness of Pound's devotion to the craft of poetry and his ideal of the impersonality of art seem, when extended over 600-odd pages, to dissipate interest instead of focusing it. The work has the hustle of artistic life, but not its inevitability. It is full of names, figures and actions; but the abiding central life of the artist judging and ordering the details, creating them in his own coherence, is not there. For all their energy and invention, their vividness and detail, despite even the devotion with which each is rendered, the *Cantos* suffer from their size and inclusiveness. It is hard to see how they "contain in themselves the reason why they are so and not otherwise". The final impression is less of artistic impersonality than of considerable casualness.

There is, in fact, a split between what is said and how

it is said, between a Flaubertian preoccupation with style and a randomness in marshalling the materials of the poem which reminds me of no method so much as the late Senator McCarthy's. For example, even in the famous Canto against usury, XLV, the feeling and the words are not quite one:

WITH USURA
wool comes not to market
sheep bringeth no gain with usura
Usura is a murrain, usura
blunteth the needle in the maid's hand
and stoppeth the spinner's cunning. Pietro Lombardo
came not by usura
Duccio came not by usura
nor Pier della Francesca; Zuan Bellin' not by usura
nor was "La Calunnia" painted.
Came not by usura Angelico; came not Ambrogio Praedis,
Came no church cut of stone signed: *Adamo me fecit.*
Not by usura St Trophime
Not by usura Saint Hilaire,
Usura rusteth the chisel
It rusteth the craft and the craftsman
It gnaweth the thread in the loom
None learneth to weave gold in her pattern;
Azure hath a canker by usura; cramoisi is unbroidered
Emerald findeth no Memling
Usura slayeth the child in the womb
It stayeth the young man's courting
It hath brought palsey to bed, lyeth
Between the young bride and her bridegroom
　　　　CONTRA NATURA
They have brought whores for Eleusis
Corpses are set to banquet
at the behest of usura.

64

It is powerful writing, but its success relies on the flow of biblical denunciation, not on the logic of the examples. The Canto has its sanction from Dante, for whom usury was also a sin against Nature and Art:

> Da queste due, se tu ti rechi a mente
> lo Genesi dal principio, conviene
> prender sua vita ed avanzar la gente.
> E perchè l'usuriere altra via tiene,
> per sè natura, e per la sua seguace
> dispregia, poichè in altro pon la spene.
> *(Inferno*, XI, 106-11)

Compared with Pound's these lines are flat; but they are reasoned, they follow out the idea. Pound ornaments it. His thought and feeling are static and separate. On one side is the rage against usury, *contra naturam*; on the other are examples of fruitfulness and culture. He writes *as though* there were a causal connection between the two, but in fact it exists only in his beliefs. And these remain simple; they are neither modified nor developed in the verse. The common ground between the belief and the examples is their appropriateness to the biblical style. The detail of the verse is elaborate and carefully wrought; the feeling is very simple.

It is this unquestioning, static quality in his beliefs that allows Pound to be satisfied at times with a surprising emotional rough-and-readiness. His inferno, for example, Cantos XIV and XV, hardly moves beyond darkness, defecation and anger. Although Dame Edith Sitwell has announced that "such lines as

Flies carrying news, harpies dripping shit through the air

are great poetry, and a living evocation of the modern

hell", I cannot see this as a Vision of Evil. It seems to me much nearer Naughtiness. It is shocking, but it is not tragic, not moral; it is nothing that involves Pound himself whether he likes it or not; it is as Henry James described Hawthorne's sense of sin: "He was not discomposed, disturbed, haunted by it in the manner of its usual and regular victims, who had not the little postern door of fancy to slip through, to the other side of the wall." For long stretches of the *Cantos* Pound holds his beliefs almost in the teeth of his poetry. He strikes a number of compromising and aggressive postures in some of the most highly disciplined and elaborate poetry of our time. It is a combination so odd that it makes the poem doubly difficult to interpret. Pound uses the ideogram: he presents isolated images, facts and anecdotes, and allows them to speak for themselves. It is left to the reader to fill in the empty spaces between them. The poet roughly insists on one interpretation; the sophisticated performance hints at another.

Hence the uneasiness of Pound's critics; it has forced them to defend the *Cantos* by slipping into explication and commentary, by pointing to the good bits and lamenting that every long poem has dull moments, or by pretending, as Mr Eliot has done, that it does not matter what Pound says; what counts is the way he says it. It seems to me that it matters very much, for it is precisely this split between belief and performance that has caused the critical shiftiness in the writing on Pound. There are two accepted masterpieces, *Mauberley* and *Propertius*; there are, I think, the equally acceptable first seven *Cantos*; and then disagreement. I cannot believe that there was any drastic change in Pound's sensibility in the early 'twenties. What happened was more consistent: he has ridden two high horses during his career, one of them popular, the other not; one had to do with cultural and poetic standards, the other was economic. I said his beliefs are simply, unquestionably held; which is to say that he has always been a writer with a cause, up to 1920 no less than after. His first cause was poetic. When he arrived in England the language and rhythms of verse were so dulled and worn they were unusable. He set about to reform them by bringing back the old standards of "Mediterranean civilization" (his phrase); these were calm, objective, rounded off and stringent. By them he could counteract both the Rhymers' self-indulgence and the utter indifference of his own "half-savage country". And in these standards he had the same absolute trust as he later put in his social remedies; even in *Mauberley* he contrasts modern Fleet Street with Dr Johnson's in a way which the author of *The Vanity of Human Wishes* would have been hard put to understand. Though the deepened, subtle tone of *Mauberley* and *Propertius* comes from the clash between belief and disenchantment, belief, in the end, won. What is so moving in the opening *Cantos* is the sense of reverence for the cultures they evoke. Pound's energy and enthusiasm brought about his reform; he made modern poetry possible.

So he turned his attention elsewhere; economic passion replaced the cultural. When he campaigned for poetic standards he did so most effectively by writing well. When he turned to social abuses he used his verse as vehicle for propaganda. The performance was no longer so inherently important. He developed a slangy, irreverent style to force over the facts. Hence the long, dull sections on Chinese and American history, Cantos LIII-LXXI, which read as though he had gone through his sources marking the bits that mattered, had gathered his findings together, but never subsequently digested them into poetry. Yet it is done with the same unwavering belief in the value of his cause. It is a belief shared by few. So the reader is constantly uneasy about what Pound will come out with next, as his sense of literature is overwhelmed by the mass of facts and theories. For his gifts are not economic; they are literary and intuitive. His most expressive form is the short poem. Both *Mauberley* and *Propertius* are a series of these; the finest parts of the *Cantos* have the same singleness and concentration. His social reforming zeal lacks the inwardness and sense of purpose that gives inevitability to a long work. In fact, the *Cantos* fail precisely when they come nearest to being a traditional long poem, when they are didactic. For the dogma he preaches and the suggestiveness of the ideogrammic method strain impossibly against each other. It is like playing a hymn-tune on a clavichord.

III

The *Pisan Cantos* are unlike Pound's other work because they were written not without a cause but from the failure of all his causes. Where in *Mauberley* and *Propertius* belief clashes with disenchantment, in the *Pisan Cantos* it disintegrates in despair. They were written when Pound was brought from his life of secluded dedication in Rapallo and put into the condemned cages at Pisa, where neither style nor theories would protect him. The result is the most extended personal verse Pound has ever written. It is personal in two ways: it is about his experiences and memories; it is also, in places, not wholly a public poem. These two elements have a great deal to do with each other. The middle sections of the *Cantos* read like a scrap-book in which much poetic material has been pasted, some with great care, some with abandon. The *Pisan Cantos* are a sort of poetic journal. The hard surface of art and fact is broken down from ideogram into tiny shards of verse in which the perennial themes of the poem jostle with memories, with details of his life in the cages and with bleak level judgments on himself:

> J'ai eu pitié des autres
> probablement pas assez, and at moments that suited my own
> convenience
> Le paradis n'est pas artificiel,
> l'enfer non plus.
> Came Eurus as comforter
> and at sunset la pastorella dei suini
> driving the pigs home, benecomata dea.   (LXXVI)

The *Pisan Cantos* are a remarkable achievement. In them Pound has moments of real impersonality: he writes of his own personal tragedy with an utter lack of self-pity. But, though it may seem a grudging verdict, they are a limited achievement; they are essentially not understandable as a whole. Their general order is that of Pound's day to day life, but their logic is the drift of his most intimate associations; it is fully available only to Pound himself. Even the ideogram breaks down, for the facts do not speak for themselves. The *Pisan Cantos*, for example, abound with names:

> and Demattia is checking out.
> White, Fazzio, Bedell, *benedicti*
> Sarnone, two Washingtons (dark) J and M
> Bassier, Starcher, H. Crowder and
> no soldier he although his name is Slaughter
> this day October the whateverth   Mr Coxie
> aged 91 has mentioned bonds and their
> > interest
> apparently as a basis of issue . . .   (LXXXIV)

None of these people are made up; Pound has repeatedly stated that he is not writing fiction in the *Cantos*. So the reader is supposed not merely to recognize them—the first lot are presumably soldiers at the camp—but to reckon up their significance. Yet Pound makes no attempt to give them any imaginative reality through action and detail. They never disengage themselves from his memories and step into the public creative world. I feel that when he abandoned *personae* and formalism he still did not achieve artistic nakedness. There is instead a despairing fragmentariness to these *Cantos*. It is as though the artistic habit were so engrafted on to him that he could avoid it only by a kind of disintegration. In the *Pisan Cantos* there is no longer any question of the life and the love being only in the learning; his effort is to make past and present, memory, experience and learning, into a living whole which will sum up the whole work. But it is the bewildering effort that comes through clearest. He succeeds in writing personally only by doing violence to the technicalities which had previously sustained

him. Yet the success in certain passages is of an order
he has not attained since 1920:

> The ant's a centaur in his dragon world.
> Pull down thy vanity, it is not man
> Made courage, or made order, or made grace,
>   Pull down thy vanity, I say pull down.
> Learn of the green world what can be thy place
> In scaled invention or true artistry,
> Pull down thy vanity,
>   Paquin pull down!
> The green casque has outdone your elegance.
>
> "Master thyself, then others shall thee beare"
>   Pull down thy vanity
> Thou art a beaten dog beneath the hail,
> A swollen magpie in a fitful sun,
> Half black half white
> Nor knowst'ou wing from tail
> Pull down thy vanity
>   How mean thy hates
> Fostered in falsity,
>   Pull down thy vanity,
> Rathe to destroy, niggard in charity,
> Pull down thy vanity,
>   I say pull down.   (LXXXI)

The whole conclusion of the *Canto*—I have quoted only
a fragment—is some of the finest sustained personal
verse that Pound has ever done. It is written too with
that same air of discovery he had in his earlier verse.
The thought again is quite simple, but it has dignity
and power. It is as though in the *Pisan Cantos* Pound
were breaking through the restrictions of craft to a
personal morality for which his earlier preoccupation

with causes had never left time. And it makes those causes seem very thin diet. The triumph of his sense of literature has been that here, in *Mauberley* and in *Propertius*, Pound's finest achievements have been to write the epitaphs on his own poetic genre.

WILLIAM EMPSON

A Style from a Despair

THE poetry of William Empson has been more used than that of any other English poet of our time. It has been more used, even, than read, for until recently it was not properly available. His early and, I think, best work appeared sporadically: there were a number of pieces in the famous *Cambridge Poetry, 1929*, which was soon wholly unobtainable; a collection appeared in 1935, and that, in turn, suffered in the same way. And so, when Empson's verse began again to be widely discussed around 1950, there was simply no full text to go on. Unless you were fortunate enough to get hold of the American edition of the *Collected Poems*, which appeared in 1949, you knew him only through his second and less exciting volume, *The Gathering Storm*, or through Michael Roberts's selection in the *Faber Book of Modern Verse*. In England the *Collected Poems* did not appear until 1955, by which time the fuss and skirmishing over the unfortunately named "Empsonians" had died down. But while it was on, most of the critics and propagandists had to rely, at best, on a feeling for their subject which they had derived from narrow, scrappy references; at worst, they were merely overwhelmed or angered by the legend of the most brilliant undergraduate poetry since Milton wrote "Il Penseroso"; they applauded or objected on principle.

So Empson's poetic discoveries themselves have not

been exploited; there is no other verse worth attention which owes as much to Empson's as, say, Cleanth Brooks's concept of "irony" owes to "ambiguity". But the poetry has been used again and again for special purposes. I. A. Richards quoted his pupil's poems in his lectures since, among other reasons, they might have been written to prove his own theory of poetry; for example, they clearly and energetically took so many other disciplines in their stride. Then a poem like "High Dive" or "Part of Mandevil's Travels" makes me think that Empson himself used his own poetry; the puns, references and provocative, open syntax seem designed to prove the value and efficacy of the critical method he used in *Seven Types*. F. R. Leavis, too, used Empson's verse. His praise at the end of *New Bearings* is part of the argument of the book. Leavis's subject was the significant reorientation of English poetry brought about by Eliot. So Empson was praised not just for his own achievement—which was qualified as "very small"—but because he had taken his bearings from Eliot and Eliot's Seventeenth Century. Ronald Bottrall was praised less guardedly for much the same reason.

In short, Empson first made his reputation as a poet as part of the movement to substantiate the important creative discoveries of the 'twenties. This is why he seems to have so little to do with the poets of the following decade, although his two volumes appeared in 1935 and 1940. His work is cool in tone, wry, controlled and unimpressed; it has no truck with the large political gestures and that fixed stare on the immediately contemporary which made up the most characteristic poetic posture before the Second World War.

It was precisely this cool, witty air which created the enthusiasm for his poetry around 1950. This time the poetry was used less to mark the way the current was running than as a reminder of the way it should run. In 1950, in the last number of *New Writing*, John Wain published an attacking essay which vigorously defined the new use Empson's work was being put to: it was an antidote against the "punch-drunk random 'romantic' scribblers" who, at that time, "occupied the poetic limelight". Empson's verse was read with an overwhelming sense of relief after the brash and embarrassed incoherence of wartime and post-war poetry. It is only fair to add that nearly all Empson's new followers were either still at the Universities or had only recently left them. They took an undergraduate delight in his tough, intellectual manner, and admired his emotional restraint because, themselves, they had slender emotional resources to draw on. Moreover, the obscurity of his verse flattered them: its allusions were either to areas they knew well already, or which were sufficiently academic to be easily mastered. (A young Harvard teacher and poet once prepared himself to review the American edition of the *Collected Poems* by tracking down every reference. In his article he announced with delight that they were all accurate and all relevant. He made it sound as though the examinee had passed something or other with distinction). The feeling was that someone had finally made convincing and original poetry out of the academic material with which these young writers were diligently loading themselves.

Finally, in Empson's refusal ever to overstate his claims, they found a precedent for their desire to have the courage of their ordinariness. Yet, though Empson may originally have been used for this end, the current sense of depressed limitation in poetry has almost nothing to do with him. Robert Conquest hardly mentioned his name in the introduction to *New Lines*, but he made a great deal of play with the influence of George Orwell's attitudes.

Empson, of course, is not responsible for his disciples. Yet there is something in his work which encourages other writers to use it for their own ends. It has, I think, an *essential* objectivity. This is not to say that it hasn't an unmistakable, individual tone, or that a great deal of personal trouble may not have gone into its making. But in the later poems what goes in as strong personal feeling comes out as something more general; whilst in the earlier work all the personal energy goes into a particularly impersonal business.

For Empson's earlier poetry is, in a way, critical. By that I do not mean that it receives its impetus from other literature, still less that it is about purely literary values, or that it is written in a style worked out beforehand and then deliberately applied. None of this. It is, rather, that the poetry is an outcome of a peculiarly strong and sensitive feeling for the intellectual tone of the time. Empson seems to create less out of personal situations than out of an emotional response to something he has already known with his wits, intellectually. His work affects you, as he said of someone else, "like a taste in the head".

In this way, Empson is a parochial poet. He is, in his poetry as well as in his criticism, the product of a particular place—Cambridge—and a particular moment —the late 'twenties—and a particular training—in a sceptical, semi-scientific tough-mindedness. His work has about it the same air of intellectual excitement as marked almost everything of the period. The strict formal disciplines—philosophy, logic and physics— had been revolutionized or, at least, given new life; in *The Sacred Wood* Eliot had begun to do the same with criticism; the development of psychology encouraged the belief that coherent, valid statements about the mind were possible—Richards even suggested that poems might eventually be evaluated scientifically, by the appetencies they satisfied. Empson, who turned from mathematics to become a pupil of Richards, has in all his work the same effort to be in all events rational, coherent and unsentimental. *Seven Types* was, among other things, an attempt to show how the effects of poetry, "so straddling an emotion and so broad a calm", had their reasons which could be discussed precisely in terms of the meanings of the words, as they were, on the page. The tone of the whole period is best summed up in the opening words of Michael Roberts' preface to the *Faber Book*: "More often than prose or mathematics poetry is received in a hostile spirit. . . ." At no other time would it have occurred to anyone that this disproportion was a subject for even the slightest surprise, still less for complaint.

The effect of this on Empson's poetry was to give him a wonderful gusto with ideas and performance. It was they that carried the emotional charge.

There is a tree native in Turkestan,
Or further east towards the Tree of Heaven,
Whose hard cold cones, not being wards to time,
Will leave their mother only for good cause;
Will ripen only in a forest fire;
Wait, to be fathered as was Bacchus once,
Through men's long lives, that image of time's end.
I knew the Phoenix was a vegetable.
So Semele desired her deity
As this in Kew thirsts for the Red Dawn.

It is odd how the tone of enquiring excitement is built up as though in the absence of the poet himself. It is as if the single scientific fact caught fire of itself and lit up all sorts of related ideas—ideas about Far Eastern, Greek, Biblical and political mythologies. They come together with a mounting grandeur, only to be doused by the off-hand summing-up:

I knew the Phoenix was a vegetable.

It is not merely a joke at the expense of the myths; it deflates the whole rhetorical tradition. For the myths are held together in a great opening seven-line sentence which uses all the traditional techniques of magniloquence: alliteration, long, open vowels and the inverted, suspended syntax of the Elizabethan grand manner. The whole thing is then punctured by the sardonic, colloquial deduction. It is done much as Liszt, I am told, used to kick the piano before concerts to show who was master. The poem has an extraordinary energy of literary sophistication, as though the poet greatly enjoyed his witty control. But something more than technical control produces the gusto:

WILLIAM EMPSON

So Semele desired her deity
As this in Kew thirsts for the Red Dawn.

In that first line Empson sounds quite as enamoured of classical mythology as Milton ever was. Yet Semele herself is not important, only the idea her situation represents. It is poetry, in fact, of the conceit; it depends on a strong feeling for ideas and a strong control over a large range of them.

In this, Empson is not as like Donne as he is usually said to be. He is far closer to the lesser Metaphysicals, to Carew or Lovelace, to Cowley or even Benlowes. That is, he is less interested in saying his own say than in the agility and skill and variety with which he juggles his ideas. So it is a personal poem only at a remove: the subject is impersonal; the involvement is all in his effort to make as much as he can out of the subject, and in the accomplishment with which he relates his manifold themes so elegantly together.

Empson's, in short, is a poetry of wit in the most traditional sense. It relies on a small audience, with much the same training and interests, who will pick up his allusions without any overemphasis on his part. And, like most wit, the pleasure it gives is largely in the immaculate performance; which is a rare pleasure but a limited one. Yeats, say, at his best demands a kind of "Ah yes" response. What is said seems so right, so naturally, economically and beautifully expressed that the poet appears not to have invented anything at all; he has merely put into its final shape some emotional truth which you already knew quite well but which had, until he reminded you of it, somehow escaped

79

formulation. On the other hand, when Empson writes on the old theme of the Coy Mistress:

> "What is conceivable can happen too,"
> Said Wittgenstein, who had not dreamt of you;

your assent is not that "Ah yes"; it is much more like Wilde's "I wish I'd said that". It is not total assent; it is admiration for the speed and the polish and the irony, for the great technical and intellectual virtuosity.

None of this implies that essential impersonality which is the mark of academic verse, verse which is not so much impersonal as dessicated. Empson's early poems have the detachment of wit, but they also have its excitement and gusto. Yet the personal involvement of the poet is oblique. This is true even of his best poem, "To an Old Lady":

> Ripeness is all; her in her cooling planet
> Revere; do not presume to think her wasted.
> Project her no projectile, plan nor man it;
> Gods cool in turn, by the sun long outlasted.
>
> Our earth alone given no name of god
> Gives, too, no hold for such a leap to aid her;
> Landing, you break some palace and seem odd;
> Bees sting their need, the keeper's queen invader.
>
> No, to your telescope; spy out the land;
> Watch while her ritual is still to see,
> Still stand her temples emptying in the sand
> Whose waves o'erthrew their crumbled tracery;
>
> Still stands uncalled-on her soul's appanage;
> Much social detail whose successor fades,
> Wit used to run a house and to play Bridge,
> And tragic fervour, to dismiss her maids.

Years her precession do not throw from gear.
She reads a compass certain of her pole;
Confident, finds no confines on her sphere,
Whose failing crops are in her sole control.

Stars how much further from me fill my night,
Strange that she too should be inaccessible,
Who shares my sun. He curtains her from sight,
And but in darkness is she visible.

Unlike most of Empson's earlier verse, this is not difficult—except for one or two minor niceties which the notes explain—and it manages to make its effect without any of those hectic intellectual contortions which provide what Empson himself called the "crossword puzzle interest" of the poems. Yet though it is a personal poem—addressed, he has said, to his mother —it succeeds not because of any particularly personal intensity. It relies, instead, on the manner in which the tone is so beautifully sustained. However much the poet seems with his subject and however large the technical equipment he brings to bear upon it, what is most striking about the poem is its tact. For essentially what he is praising in the old lady is her decorum, her sense of style:

Wit used to run a house and to play Bridge,
And tragic fervour, to dismiss her maids.

It has that serious ironic admiration for style that is like Pope's (I once thought that "used" was not the past participle, meaning "employed", but part of the imperfect tense; and this made it sound more like Pope than ever, for "Wit" and "tragic fervour" then became personifications). Hence the old lady can be observed, meditated on, admired, but finally she is "inaccessible". The poem has reverence, but it is for a way of life that has become remote, for a style. In short, "To an Old Lady" derives its energy from a source which, however heightened and dignified it may be, is still that of his other work: a powerful feeling for the depths and intricacies of manners. His best early poems—"To an Old Lady", "This Last Pain", "Arachne", "The Ants", "Invitation to Juno", "Camping Out", "Note on Local Flora" and "Legal Fiction"—contrive to make up an extraordinary personal achievement without risking any properly personal statement. Instead, they are acts of the most subtle critical reverence to the whole concept, style. Perhaps in this Empson was more alive than any of his contemporaries to the implications of Eliot's poetic innovations.

Empson's preoccupation with style, however, occasionally lapsed into a preoccupation with the tricks of meaning. He spoke of this, in a dissatisfied way, as his "clotted style", and in "Bacchus" he reduced it to its unreadable conclusion: the notes were about twice the length of the poem. The intellectual toughness had developed, to say the least, into a mannerism.

Since Empson had always avoided exaggerating his personal claims, it was appropriate that he should also avoid exaggerating his style. The tone of the second volume, *The Gathering Storm*, was a good deal clearer. But this was the result of a change of emphasis, not of heart. Instead of elaborate verbal contortions, the new manner reduced the poetry to bare statements which were forced into profundity by being juxtaposed one with the other:

All losses haunt us. It was a reprieve
Made Dostoevsky talk out queer and clear.

Those stay most haunting that most soon deceive

And turn out no loss of the various Zoo
The public spirits or the private play . . .

The pieces have just enough emotional coherence to
make the argument tantalizing and just too little to
make it inevitable. So, despite the superficial clarity,
the reader has to work quite as hard as with the earlier
"puzzle" style.

It was typical of this new emphasis that in the most
technically original of these poems, "The Teasers",
Empson discovered a way of writing complex poetry
almost without metaphor. He did it by a kind of
grammatical stutter which fixed attention upon those
thin, weightless little words which are normally hardly
noticed:

Not but they die, the teasers and the dreams,
Not but they die . . .

The poem was difficult although it had few of the usual
puzzles of metaphor or argument or reference. It
seemed to have transferred to the realm of personal
poetry the kind of linguistic interest normally reserved
for modern philosophers.

The new style, however, meant unequivocally that
Empson no longer found his earlier elegance satisfying.
The important thing was now to state his own personal
conclusions. Earlier, the energy and conviction had
gone into marshalling his ideas and into his superb
intellectual rhetoric; now, by an effort of formidable

technical concentration, the personal experience became generalized into ideas. For example, the best and the best known of the later poems, "Missing Dates":

> Slowly the poison the whole blood stream fills.
> It is not the effort nor the failure tires.
> The waste remains, the waste remains and kills.
>
> It is not your system or clear sight that mills
> Down small to the consequence a life requires;
> Slowly the poison the whole blood stream fills.
>
> They bled an old dog dry yet the exchange rills
> Of young dog blood gave but a month's desires
> The waste remains, the waste remains and kills.
>
> It is the Chinese tombs and the slag hills
> Usurp the soul, and not the soil retires.
> Slowly the poison the whole blood stream fills.
>
> Not to have fire is to be a skin that shrills.
> The complete fire is death. From partial fires
> The waste remains, the waste remains and kills.
>
> It is the poems you have lost, the ills
> From missing dates, at which the heart expires.
> Slowly the poison the whole blood stream fills.
> The waste remains, the waste remains and kills.

It is a famous and convincing poem, and doubtless the product of much suffering. But there is a curiously static quality about it. It has none of that swarming logical drive which did so much to keep the early poems in motion; for example, the "old dog" and the "Chinese tombs" are merely plainly stated examples; they do not develop the generalizations, nor make them more flexible. Then there is the heavy, flat rhythm, which is apt enough for the subject of the poem—the inevitability of defeat—but which works like a drug; it deadens you into accepting the resigned emptiness, but spares you the more personal difficulty of feeling the poet's conclusions out for yourself. There is no question of the tone being forced or false; but the real poem seems to have happened before the actual poem, as it is on the page, was written. That is, all the conflict and regret and resignation have gone into producing the two key lines of the villanelle:

Slowly the poison the whole blood stream fills. . . .
The waste remains, the waste remains and kills. . . .

As the poem unwinds, these generalizations are clarified, but they are not intensified. They are transformed almost into abstractions, ideas to be proved, commented on, illustrated, but no longer to be felt out. For the feeling has happened before the poem started, and from it the poet had produced two working hypotheses as a kind of test for everything else that is said. Even the beautiful closing lines seem rather to clinch the generalizations Empson began with than to transform them into something new.

It is this static quality that distinguishes the later verse from the early. The poems in *The Gathering Storm* are less specialized than those of the first volume; they are, in a way, more applicable and more serious; but they lack that sense of potentiality and triumphant elegance. In the early poems the ideas were constantly expanding one into another controlled by a powerful and ironic logic; but it was a tentative control. The poems came to rest in a kind of temporary balance of their forces, as though in the teeth of all possible complexities the poet had managed to substantiate, at least, a style. In his sardonic way, Empson made his polish and inventiveness seem like a personal claim for sanity, as though he saw everything in a fourth and horrifying dimension but was too well-mannered to say so. Hence the wry despair and vigorous stylishness seemed not at all contradictory. On the other hand, the later poems seem to be less personal discoveries than expansions of the passage from the Fire Sermon which Empson has put at the front of the *Collected Poems*:

> . . . Knowing this, Bhikkhus, the wise man, . . . becomes weary of the eye, he becomes weary of the visible, he becomes weary of the knowledge of the visible, he becomes weary of the contact of the visible, he becomes weary of the feeling which arises from the contact of the visible, be it pleasure, be it pain, be it neither pleasure nor pain . . .

No doubt, to understand this from the inside was far beyond Empson's ken when he was younger, and to present his understanding with such impersonal deliberation is still beyond the ken of nearly all of his contemporaries. Yet what the poems have gained in general truth they have lost in stylish and enquiring originality. And it is as a stylist of poetry and ideas that, I think, Empson is most important. He took over all Eliot's hints about what was most significant in the English tradition, and he put them into practice without any of the techniques Eliot had derived from the French and Italians. And so his poetry shows powerfully and with great purity the perennial vitality of the English tradition; and in showing this it also expresses the vitality and excitement of the extraordinarily creative moment when Empson began writing.

86

W. H. AUDEN

Poetry and Journalism

We are forlorn like children, and experienced like old men,
we are crude and sorrowful and superficial—I believe we
are lost.
 Erich Maria Remarque, "All Quiet on the Western
 Front"

ENGLISH literature now, in the 1950s, is safely back
 on the track that seemed to have been abandoned
 when *Prufrock and Other Observations* appeared in
1917; it is back in the old way of traditional forms,
traditional language and more or less traditional sentiments. It has got there, I think, not as a reaction to the
incoherence of the 'forties, nor through the influence
of William Empson's poetry—which, after all, seems
to owe a great deal to Eliot and his critical texts—but
by way of the work of Auden and his poetic colleagues
of the 'thirties. Auden himself, as an undergraduate
poet, was obviously influenced by Eliot, but there is
essentially almost nothing in common between them.
Auden has never had time for that formal, aesthetic
preoccupation of Eliot and Pound, that dandified
elegance and precision in their use of language, which
is part explained by their intimate relationship with
Gautier and the French Symbolists, and part by their
air of having to work out *a priori* for themselves a
poetic language to suit their complex and learned
sensibilities. Auden does not have that kind of profound
originality. Where Eliot transformed the sensibility of

his age, Auden caught the tone of his. And his age was clever, knowing, and rather suspicious of too much interest in "the art of poetry". Louis MacNeice once claimed that the poets of the 'thirties had more important things to do than to be highly cultivated and esoteric. He meant their political commitments. And perhaps there is in Auden's work an element of what might be called writing for the proletariat: he says what he has to say without much difficulty, and then, of course, he never has anything very difficult to say. His business was, and still is, to catch the tone of the time, and he has done so by filling out traditional forms and metres with an off-hand, up-to-date language. I imagine that in a hundred years or so Auden will indeed be difficult. But his obscurity is only skin-deep. Notes to his works will be like those to *The Dunciad* or to the *Cantos*, explaining the topical allusions, the figures, the events, the slang phrases. They won't much affect the profundity of the work.

Though ease and fluency are as essential to his style as polish is to Wallace Stevens's, Auden has without any doubt written too much. In the great mass of his work there is no sharp line between the fluent and the prattling, the easy and the void. He is not voluminous because he has published his experiments; the failures are all remarkably alike and uneventful. His work, in fact, is rarely tentative, but it is often very monotonous. His failures have a slickness which lives parasitically off the trimness and speed of his better work. He has, in short, published a great deal of verse which, like Byron's tales, seems to have been written while dressing for dinner.

His failures are not only of the same type, they are mostly on the same theme. Quite simply, Auden has never written, by the standards of his own best work, a good personal poem. And by "personal" I mean something of the order of Yeats's "A Deep-Sworn Vow":

> Others because you did not keep
> That deep-sworn vow have been friends of mine;
> Yet always when I look death in the face,
> When I clamber to the heights of sleep,
> Or when I grow excited with wine,
> Suddenly I meet your face.

It may well be that Auden hasn't the kind of machinery that can do a thing as simple as that. But then "A Deep-Sworn Vow" is simple only in language. The firm generosity which holds together regret and irony in all their fullness is anything but simple. It must have cost the poet a great deal of strength to achieve anything as lucid as that. It is precisely that strength which is lacking in Auden's most often quoted love lyric, where fullness is confused with emphatic gesture:

> Lay your sleeping head, my love,
> Human on my faithless arm;
> Time and fevers burn away
> Individual beauty from
> Thoughtful children, and the grave
> Proves the child ephemeral:
> But in my arms till break of day
> Let the living creature lie,
> Mortal, guilty, but to me
> The entirely beautiful . . .

I suppose the balance, like the feelings, is meant to be precarious, swaying between the full and the knowing, between "The entirely beautiful" and "Human on my faithless arm". But there is a kind of vague, generalized feeling to the verse, as though Auden were writing a love poem to someone he had never been properly introduced to. Those "Thoughtful children" were, after all, part of the emotional shorthand of the time, like Auden's own "impetuous child with the tremendous brain" and those inhumanly brilliant children in *Eyeless in Gaza*. Compared with the actors in "Among School Children" and "A Prayer for My Daughter" they hardly seem to be children at all. Instead, they are ciphers for a sad, but half-hearted and almost modish yearning.

Auden, of course, has written successful poems which are almost personal, in the accepted sense: Prospero's opening speech in *The Sea and the Mirror*, or "A Summer Night 1933" are excellent in their inventive, easygoing, allusive way; but both are personal at the removes of, respectively, a mask and an occasion. When he has only himself and perhaps one other person to talk about both feelings and sense of style disappear into an elaborate coyness ("Shut Your Eyes and Open Your Mouth", for example) or into the fog of a morning-after despair:

> Tempus fugit. Quite.
> So finish up your drink.

I would not have mentioned these more intimate pieces at all, had they not been so many. They show only that the difficult balance of personal statement is not among Auden's many talents.

But when he can use appropriately a lighter and

more swinging rhythm, or when he has a subject he can set about from the outside, the work picks up life; it becomes tenser and fuller—and so, in a way, more personal. For all the poet's interests seem to be engaged; and they are those of the skilled and critical technician, whose raw material is made up of certain rather specialized insights.

Perhaps his most typical product is "Consider"; it needs to be quoted in full:

> Consider this and in our time
> As the hawk sees it or the helmeted airman:
> The clouds rift suddenly—look there
> At cigarette-end smouldering on a border
> At the first garden party of the year.
> Pass on, admire the view of the massif
> Through plate-glass windows of the Sport Hotel;
> Join there the insufficient units
> Dangerous, easy, in furs, in uniform
> And constellated at reserved tables
> Supplied with feelings by an efficient band
> Relayed elsewhere to farmers and their dogs
> Sitting in kitchens in the stormy fens.
>
> Long ago, supreme Antagonist,
> More powerful than the great northern whale
> Ancient and sorry at life's limiting defect,
> In Cornwall, Mendip, or the Pennine moor
> Your comments on the highborn mining-captains,
> Found they no answer, made them wish to die
> —Lie since in barrows out of harm.
> You talk to your admirers every day
> By silted harbours, derelict works,
> In strangled orchards, and the silent comb
> Where dogs have worried or a bird was shot.

Order the ill that they attack at once:
Visit the ports and, interrupting
The leisurely conversation in the bar
Within a stone's throw of the sunlit water,
Beckon your chosen out. Summon
Those handsome and diseased youngsters, those women
Your solitary agents in the country parishes;
And mobilize the powerful forces latent
In soils that make the farmer brutal
In the infected sinus, and the eyes of stoats.
Then, ready, start your rumour, soft
But horrifying in its capacity to disgust
Which, spreading magnified, shall come to be
A polar peril, a prodigious alarm,
Scattering the people, as torn-up paper
Rags and utensils in a sudden gust,
Seized with immeasurable neurotic dread.

Seekers after happiness, all who follow
The convolutions of your simple wish,
It is later than you think; nearer that day
Far other than that distant afternoon
Amid rustle of frocks and stamping feet
They gave the prizes to the ruined boys.
You cannot be away, then, no
Not though you pack to leave within an hour,
Escaping humming down arterial roads:
The date was yours; the prey to fugues,
Irregular breathing and alternate ascendancies
After some haunted migratory years
To disintegrate on an instant in the explosion of mania
Or lapse for ever into a classic fatigue.

The poem reminds me of one of those Elizabethan
plays scholars wrangle about—*Doctor Faustus*, for

instance. Part of it has genius, part is hack-work. And like *Doctor Faustus*, the two parts have precious little to do with each other. The good bits—they stand out—— are almost entirely of one type; their strength is that of accuracy and economy:

> . . . And constellated at reserved tables
> Supplied with feelings by an efficient band
> Relayed elsewhere to farmers and their dogs
> Sitting in kitchens in the stormy fens.

Or most of the last section, particularly:

> . . . that distant afternoon
> Amid rustle of frocks and stamping feet
> They gave the prizes to the ruined boys.

The lines are founded on business-like observation and a wonderful sense of language. When Auden is writing seriously and well there is rarely any question of his liking his subjects; he merely guts them as neatly as a fishwife deals with a herring. Behind his best work is a tradition that reached its peak with:

> Where slumber abbots purple as their wines.

This is not just a gift for destructive criticism; there is relish and vitality in the performance of a writer who is without doubt very clever, and who enjoys the business of using his skill to let in a little air. But still, the strength is in the accuracy of the observation; it is a flair for the telling detail as well as the telling word. If Auden is contemporary (and he seems to me much more "contemporary" than "modern", with all that last word, in its best sense, implies of profound originality), he is so in the way a journalist is contemporary. That is, his business is to observe accurately, to present succinctly and to comment. His comment should be pointed, it should be allusive to what is happening there and then, to fashionable ideas and theories; but within these limits it should be easy. The journalist is not, in short, ever called on to think particularly painfully. His business is with the surface of things, not with their real nature. Even Auden's prose, which is very lively and knock-you-down, is more a matter of quick and deft juggling with received ideas—from psychology, anthropology, sociology, and so on—than any real effort to get at something he knows, however obscurely, for himself. If Pope is on one side of Auden, Alistair Cook is on the other.

It is also the journalist in him who allows Auden so much freedom of the cliché. Set beside the lines over which he really seems to have taken pains, large stretches of the poem appear to have been botched up with whatever catch-phrases were nearest to hand:

> . . . The insufficient units. . . .

> . . . Silted harbours, derelict works. . . .

> . . . Scattering the people, as torn-up paper
> Rags and utensils in a sudden gust. . . .

They are all phrases from that Thesaurus of Social Abuses which became so thumb-marked during the 'thirties. It is as though Auden had not written the lines at all, but merely compiled them. This is quite another thing from a poet's making, by over-use, a cliché of his own original discoveries, as Wordsworth did in his decline, and as Eliot has done in his 1954

Ariel Poem. These at least give you the feeling that
they once meant something; if they are no longer fresh,
that is because the poet himself has stopped discovering.
But Auden's clichés are quite general, stuck on to the
scene automatically, and only remotely connected with
the poet himself. It is, of course, perfectly possible to
inject a little life into a spent phrase; Pound has done so
often enough, triumphantly in *Mauberley*. But he only
managed it by using them ironically for his own ends.
There are no inverted commas, metaphorical or real,
around Auden's clichés; they are obviously intended
as serious and moving poetry. Just how much they fail
and how inert they are, he himself shows:

> By silted harbours, derelict works,
> In strangled orchards, and the silent comb
> Where dogs have worried or a bird was shot.

It is extraordinary how that last line and a half make
you attend; a whole area of allusion wakes into life after
the lethargy that has gone before. The movement of the
verse becomes more subtle; the poet is no longer shift-
ing around the required properties; in fact, he is less
describing the actual scene than registering its importance on him. On the evidence of the poetry, I can't
really believe that social abuses ever much troubled
Auden, though they may at one time have excited him.
But he does seem to have had a profound *odi-et-amo*
relationship with the tougher squirearchy, who control
with real power their tiny estates in the bleaker parts of
England. Hence some of Auden's best writing appears
in the very early *Paid On Both Sides*, in which, with the
aid of *Beowulf*, he raised his passion for private games

and his otherwise overworked sense of doom almost to the level of moral statement. It is as though he yearned for authority in action whilst rejecting it in control. And so there is a curious ambivalence in his attitude to money and power; he says they won't do and yet he has a romantic yearning for those graced with them. There was once an exchange between Scott Fitzgerald and Hemingway that has now achieved notoriety: "The rich", said Fitzgerald, "are different from us." "Yes", replied the good democrat, "they have more money." Time and again Auden's poetry seems to be repeating these sentiments—but taking both sides at once:

Dangerous, easy, in furs, in uniform. . .

I can't quite understand how Auden manages to take the international set so seriously. They are self-seeking, superficial, and possibly, at best, cunning. But "dangerous"? Even from the party line they were mere riff-raff to be swept away. Yet somehow the poet has made of them a personal menace.

For Auden is a journalist not only in the type of social observation he can do and in his freedom with the cliché; there is also his sensationalism. This is why the moments of brilliant social comment are not apparently enough. There has to be a sort of Q.E.D. structure; society must die of its own disease, a rebellion of some undefined sort must take place, and finally his own personal dislikes must go under. So in the second section of the poem an enormous machinery of Fate is rumbled into motion, with full Anglo-Saxon trappings and an obscure mythology to go with it (that "great northern whale", for example; if he is immortal, then he can't be an ordinary whale; whilst Moby Dick, my only other candidate, had his hunting grounds mostly in the southern hemisphere). The aim seems to be to create a sort of modern epic, complete with a modern hero—"the hawk . . . or the helmeted airman"—in which heroic action and Fate will combine to purge society. But somehow the social revolution is lost in the nerves. The poem ends not in the triumph of political right, or of any sort of right, but in psychosis:

> To disintegrate on an instant in the explosion of mania
> Or lapse for ever into a classic fatigue.

I am told that Auden believed that the corruption of society was reflected in the nervous disorder of the people. Perhaps. But then the dread and ominousness of social revolution seem to me considerably worked up, out of proportion to the incisiveness of the start and not quite *à propos* of the theme. For what the dissatisfied, the warped and the diseased have to do with the purgation of society is by no means clear. Certainly no political leader would own them. Even the *intellectual* Marxists have always been rather an embarrassment to Moscow.

Granted "Consider" is not a straight political poem, like "Spain" or the much better "A Summer Night 1933"—even its title shows it to be an analysis of a country rotten with its own ingrown triviality—nevertheless the machinery of inevitability rumbles away and the catch phrases are used. So it does have a certain political air. The difficulty is to see what the moments of satire and of Fate have to do with each other, for the change from one to the other is muffled and rather underhand. In the second section the emotions are worked up almost blindly, ending in a loud and unconvincing rhetorical outburst.

If I am hard put to know what exactly the poem is at, it is not only because it has the air of having been written by two hands, the real poet and the hack; there is also the split between sureness and fantasy. While either end of the poem is detached and deadly accurate, the central section is a blur of ominousness and threat, like a child telling a horror story; he manages to frighten himself without ever quite knowing what the horror is. My own impression is that it has little to do with the social detail. What is being aired is one single man's terror of guilt and retribution, not that of a whole society. For there is little difference between the feelings that motivate the central section of "Consider" and those of "The Witnesses":

> You are the town and We are the clock.
> We are the guardians of the gate in the rock.
>   The Two.
> On your left and on your right
> In the day and in the night,
>   We are watching you.
>
> Wiser not to ask just what has occurred
> To them who disobeyed our word;
>   To those
> We were the whirlpool, we were the reef,
> We were the formal nightmare, grief
>   And the unlucky rose.
>
> Climb up the crane, learn the sailor's words
> When the ships from the islands laden with birds
>   Come in;

Tell you stories of fishing and other men's wives,
The expansive dreams of constricted lives,
    In the lighted inn.

But do not imagine We do not know,
Or that what you hide with such care won't show
    At a glance:
Nothing is done, nothing is said,
But don't make the mistake of believing us dead;
    I shouldn't dance.

We're afraid in that case you'll have a fall;
We've been watching you over the garden wall
    For hours:
The sky is darkening like a stain;
Something is going to fall like rain,
    And it won't be flowers.

When the green field comes off like a lid,
Revealing what was much better hid—
    Unpleasant:
And look, behind you without a sound
The woods have come up and are standing round
    In deadly crescent.

The bolt is sliding in its groove;
Outside the window is the black remov-
    -er's van:
And now with sudden swift emergence
Come the hooded women, the hump-backed surgeons,
    And the Scissor Man.

This might happen any day;
So be careful what you say
    And do:
Be clean, be tidy, oil the lock,
Weed the garden, wind the clock;
    Remember the Two.

The real difference between the two poems is that this latter is wholly successful. Where "Consider" is muddled by a kind of poetic journalism—another name for superficiality—in "The Witnesses" this sensationalism is directly exploited. The result is some of the most effective and disturbing light verse since *The Hunting of the Snark*. And in light verse the first requirements are that its effect be immediate and its direction straightforward. The details do not have to lead towards any profound insight, they have only to be striking and lively. Because "Consider" seems to be attempting more, it demands proportionately closer attention; sooner or later you have to ask what, for example, the diseased have to do with the reform of society. But who cares what the unlucky rose is, what exactly will fall like rain, or why the crescent is deadly? It is enough that the swing of the thing carries it over. And it carries it all in the same direction:

> When the green field comes off like a lid,
> Revealing what was much better hid—
>   Unpleasant . . .

> The bolt is sliding in its groove . . .

> Come the hooded women, the hump-backed surgeons,
>   And the Scissor Man . . .

The unison to all this is in the horrors of neurotic fantasy. Behind it looms the figure of Straw Peter.

The sureness and invention show that Auden knows precisely what he is about. And any analyst could run through this collection of images without a moment's pause. So there is in the poem an element of game and deliberate manipulation. But it is no less effective for that. The disturbance comes through unhindered. All that the poet has avoided is the need to say anything about it or, having expressed it, to do anything further with it. He does not, in short, have to think with any particular rigour. The images, well chosen, powerfully expressed and ingeniously ordered though they are, are all of the surface of the mind. He never makes the step beyond them, inwards, towards personal meaning. Without doubt the personal meaning *may* be there; the images *may* have very specific meaning for the poet. But it is not insisted on; no one image is followed up to its source; they are merely drawn up smartly in formation and marched off purposefully at the double. The enemy is not mentioned, but it is obvious who and where he is.

Auden is particularly good at this sort of briskness and efficiency. They say he can turn out any form of verse at well-nigh a moment's notice. He can also deal with any subject or occasion, provided it does not touch him too closely, or, if it does, provided he does not have to treat it seriously. And so in the *Collected Shorter Poems* the section entitled "Songs and Other Musical Pieces" is infinitely more successful as a whole than any of the others. Once, in the introduction to his excellent anthology, *The Oxford Book of Light Verse*, Auden seemed to excuse his praise of the genre by a kind of political conviction:

> A democracy in which each citizen is as fully conscious and capable of making a rational choice, as in the past has been possible only for the wealthier few, is the only kind of society which in the future is likely to survive for long.

In such a society, and in such alone, will it be possible for the poet, without sacrificing any of his subtleties of sensibility or his integrity, to write poetry which is simple, clear, and gay.

For poetry which is at the same time light and adult can only be written in a society which is both integrated and free.

This was written, incidentally, just before he left for America. Perhaps his idealism may be justified. None of us is in a position to know. But Auden's own preference for light verse begins, I think, more simply from the fact that he is so good at it. It allows room for all his technical skill and buoyancy, his knowingness, ingenuity, and speed with a phrase or a reference. Although in the same introduction he claimed that "Light verse can be serious", it is not so with the deep, exploratory seriousness of an original knowledge of experience. And no one would ever want it to be. There is a basic, easy-going impersonality in light verse, like the rules of a game. The first need of the poet is to keep the thing going with vigour. He must fit his ends and his invention to the pattern.

Auden, in fact, is one of those poets who, in order to write well, needs an impersonal occasion and a strict form. For this reason he has always seemed so much more at home in traditional metres accommodated to contemporary speech than with the more subtle inward movements which Eliot and Lawrence evolved to cope with the isolated complexities of their sensibilities. Of all twentieth-century poets Auden would feel most at home in the age of Dryden, the age of informed, satiric and slightly gossipy occasional verse.

As the seventeenth century read sermons more or less for pleasure, so the twentieth has devoted itself religiously to critical essays. I am afraid that the bulk of them will eventually prove as unreadable as the sermons. But criticism is at least a mode that has suited Auden's particular talents. A number of his better poems are, in a peculiarly concise and epigrammatic form, literary essays: for example, "Musée des Beaux Arts", "Voltaire at Ferney", "In Memory of W. B. Yeats", "To E. M. Forster", "Matthew Arnold", "Edward Lear", "Pascal", "Rimbaud", "In Memory of Ernst Toller", "At the Grave of Henry James", "Herman Melville" and "In Memory of Sigmund Freud". Indeed, Auden's last good poem, *The Sea and the Mirror*, is a brilliant and convincing modernization of *The Tempest*— although I wish he had not confused Caliban with Kenneth Burke. Like all his best poems, these have an impersonal framework, a subject to which he must accommodate himself. Hence there is a decorum imposed on what he can say. He does not in fact always observe it. At times he can be as silly in his critical poems as in his personal: of Voltaire, for instance:

> Dear Diderot was dull but did his best;
> Rousseau, he'd always known, would blubber and give in.

But at very least the poems are used to put over an idea about another writer. And Auden's ideas, whatever else can be said about them, are always bright.

For example, both he and Hart Crane wrote poems about Melville. Auden begins:

> Towards the end he sailed into an extraordinary mildness,
> And anchored in his home and reached his wife
> And rode within the harbour of her hand,
> And went across each morning to the office
> As though his occupation were another island.

And Crane:

> Often beneath the wave, wide from this ledge
> The dice of drowned men's bones he saw bequeath
> An embassy. Their numbers as he watched,
> Beat on the dusty shore and were obscured.

It is a question of the kind of response each requires. To the neatness and appropriateness of Auden's metaphor you give the adherence that comes of delighted recognition: "That's a good way of putting it!" The ingenuity is persuasive; in the end, the poet has succeeded if you accept his interpretation; it is more a matter of the intellect than of the emotions. Crane's poem, on the other hand, is only nominally attached to its subject. It is primarily about himself and the sea; Melville is its excuse. Nevertheless, it is undeniably a poem; it works on you obscurely, whether you like it or not; agreement is not at all in question. It is as though Crane were stating a fact about himself—to refute it would be to misunderstand—while Auden is discussing a subject quite outside himself. Crane, in this instance, is writing poetry, Auden verse. For verse is a means and poetry an end.

But Auden is a master of verse—and a master only with verse. He can almost never do without this third element: the impersonal point of reference to which he directs the reader. It does not much matter whether this is society, literature, mythology or politics, or whether it is the subtle and elaborate game of serious light verse. Once he has an impersonal framework his real gifts come into action: his technical inventiveness, his striking but scrappy ideas, his great range of reading, his wit and, above all, his superb command of language.

These are rare gifts, stimulating and admirable. Yet somehow I can't, in the real sense, *agree* with Auden as I agree with Lawrence and Yeats. What he has positively to offer does not seem to matter much. I cannot, that is, get much from his work beyond the extraordinary ability and cleverness. He has caught one tone of his period, but it is a cocktail party tone, as though most of his work were written off the cuff for the amusement of his friends. No doubt much of it was, and at times this tone is right—in social or literary comment, or in light verse. It is when he tries to write seriously without these supports that he falls flat. When it is just a matter of saying his say without satire or bounce he seems emotionally puny or lopsided. And so his seriousness merges into a too-easy sensationalism. No doubt the sense of impending disaster in the 'thirties was oppressive; but what actually happened after 1939 was so much more appalling than anyone imagined that all the talk of nerves, injustice and retribution now appears trivial. It was Orwell who pointed out that Auden could never have written as he did about the Spanish Civil War had he really known what it was like. This is true *a fortiori* of everything he had to say of the situation which led up to the Second World War. It seems as little to the purpose as was Rupert Brooke's heroism. When in Auden the disturbance does break convincingly through—in "The Witnesses", for example—it not only bears very indirectly on his political themes, but has every appearance of being so upsetting that, if it were not set to work churning out brilliant light verse, it might overwhelm him completely. So he has the strained, almost excruciated air of a man with his arm in a hole in a dyke, who is pretending all the while that he is merely lounging there to enjoy the sun and chat with passers-by.

To put it another way: the work of the great poets adds up to more than the sum of their individual poems. Each poem has an intricate but organic relationship to a whole interpretation of experience. This is true of the great poets of tradition, and it is true in our own time of Lawrence, Eliot and Yeats. For at the centre of all of them is a core of knowledge which, though it is continually extended, never essentially alters; for they have made the creative effort to know and judge their own experience; from the sureness of this they move outwards again to know and judge the experience of their time. At the centre of Auden's work, on the other hand, I can find only a kind of nervous blankness. His best work is, compared with that of the others, peripheral, a poetry of technique, brilliant critical insights and ingenuity. He revived all the traditional means and accommodated them to a resolutely contemporary language. In this way he caught once and for all the tone of a particular time and a particular circle. But the tone was naturally transitory and the moment has passed.

THE LYRIC OF HART CRANE

*Ah ça! voici qui est plaisant: depuis que je dois mourir tous
les vers que j'ai jamais sus en ma vie me reviennent à la
mémoire. Ce sera un signe de décadence. . . .*
STENDHAL, "Le Rouge et le Noir"

THE myth of tortured genius and the related cult
of exacerbated sensibility have done Crane's
reputation great harm. Those who believe in it
have loaded Crane with a greatness which weighs down
his real, and more slender talent. Those who resist it
accuse Crane of inflated, rhetorical effusions and more
than his fair share of poetic luck. Either way, he comes
out badly. He is clearly not a great epic genius; equally
clearly, he wrote some good and original poems. It was
Crane himself who believed blindly in genius. There
seems no reason to think that he knew very precisely
what sort of genius he had.

For the main element of his life was confusion. There
was the artistic confusion of his tradition: he thought of
himself as descending from both Whitman *and* Poe; he
was "influenced" in the dangerous, superficial way by
all the reading Eliot made fashionable: the Metaphysicals, the French Symbolists, the Jacobean dramatists, Blake. From them he took hints about language,
but missed their intellectual taste. He wrote, when he
was not working at advertising copy, during the confusion of the most pretentious Greenwich Village experimentation. From all this he tried to forge an epic
style. He lived out his confusions personally: his

parents were constantly quarrelling, viciously possessive and finally divorced; his father, a candy manufacturer from Ohio, thought poetry hateful, soft and unsafe; Crane never completed his education; he was an alcoholic and a homosexual. He committed suicide in 1932, when he was in his early 30s.

Against this, he had on his side a superb ear, great sensitivity to language and an awareness which, though it lacked breadth, went deep. His sensibility was restricted to the minutiae of his reactions. It left little room for reason and not much more for observation. He worked above all by spontaneity; constriction, or whatever we would call the rational part of communication, he disregarded.

Yet he tried to write an epic. Crane seems to have been a man of few ideas but strong beliefs. He believed intensely in the absolute quality of poetic language, that the poet, inspired, could do no wrong. Which is not to say that he was careless; he revised and rewrote a great deal. But his standard was always richness of texture and concentration, never plainness. I will return to this. What matters here is that an epic in this style would be difficult to maintain and even harder to orientate. Crane's other riding belief was more common and more pernicious. He got into his head the idea of the great American poem, the poem which should create the myth of the U.S.A. from its legends, history and its present scene. He thought he could do this by spanning all his topics by his single imaginative symbol, the Bridge. *The Bridge*, however, is coherent only in its theory. It is a symbol of the poem Crane wanted to write; it has no real life apart from his creative will.

Crane's tragedy is that he was never able to let be. He never really got over the idea of the great American poem. The feeling that he was written out, which is said to have driven him into suicide, was, I believe, brought about by the failure of *The Bridge* as an epic. It was praised far more highly than his earlier volume, *White Buildings*, but it was praised as a collection of lyrics. Even his friend Allen Tate complained of its "fragmentary and often unintelligible framework". And Crane was haunted by this sense of limited greatness. Yet it was precisely because he belonged so much to his age and place that he failed to write the great long American poem, yet always, whatever his theme, wrote American poetry. For he inherited the chaos of his time; he reacted violently and, in the end, tragically, against Middle West philistinism; he thought of himself as moving along an opposite and more native path than the one Eliot's cosmopolitan intelligence followed; he held his own ground and his own themes when all his friends were deserting to the exiled cliques of Paris. His Americanism was a central part of his genius; greatness was not. In this way he is like Scott Fitzgerald: he responded so fully to his time that he could never go beyond its limitations. His isolation itself and that sense he gives of someone always swimming against the tide helps to define the area of his work. It is nearly always a matter of effort; which is not necessarily a mark of excellence, but it has helped create that effect of dusty grandeur which has encouraged so many critics to call him "a great failure".

Towards the end of his life Crane, too, came to think of himself in this way. His suicide was almost his mark of approval of the label. But he too wanted for his genius something it did not have. Judged by the standards of epic greatness, his failure is not in doubt. He lacked altogether the authority and stamina which come from a firm moral and poetic tradition. His religion was a vague Ouspensky mysticism and his epic standard was largely Whitman's vatic outpouring. By saying that he lacked this central control and stability I am in fact denying him the qualities not merely of a great epic poet but of a *great* poet in any sense. If Crane failed, it was not to achieve greatness, but because he let the idea of greatness hound him into denying his own gifts. Like Marvell, Crane is not a writer who failed to do great things; he is, instead, a fine minor poet—to my mind, one of the best American poets of the century. He lacks the wit and temperance of Wallace Stevens, but he has a more vivid range of experience; he has, too, a serious originality that is rare anywhere. But it is the range and originality of a lyric poet.

Poetry, in a rough, working simplification, is of two types: discursive and intuitive. The former relies on the pressure of reason to order and stabilize its various elements. It is founded on a belief in the intellectual coherence of experience; it attains its balance and inclusiveness by a questing, worrying rationalism that will not let the subject be. This is Eliot's mode. Intuitive poetry—the lyric—is slighter. It rises from a single, intense moment of perception and concerns the poet's reactions to the object, rather than the object itself. Discursive poetry starts from the transitory, measures it and builds upon it. Lyric poetry records it as it is.

Someone has pointed out that in Blake's *Sunflower*, for instance, there is no main verb. There is no need of one. The whole poem is only an expansion of the single feeling "Ah sunflower . . ." This is how Crane worked. He depends entirely on the spontaneity of his reactions and on his ability to fit words to them so as to leave the smallest possible gap between the language and the feelings. There is rarely any readily paraphrasable content, any argument to be realized and discussed. His poems either feel right or they don't. For example, the Proem to his epic, *The Bridge*:

> How many dawns, chill from his rippling rest
> The seagull's wings shall dip and pivot him,
> Shedding white rings of tumult, building high
> Over the chained bay waters Liberty—
>
> Then, with inviolate curve, forsake our eyes
> As apparitional as sails that cross
> Some page of figures to be filed away;
> —Till elevators drop us from our day . . .
>
> I think of cinemas, panoramic sleights
> With multitudes bent toward some flashing scene
> Never disclosed, but hastened to again,
> Foretold to other eyes on the same screen;
>
> And Thee, across the harbour, silver-paced
> As though the sun took step of thee, yet left
> Some motion ever unspent in thy stride,—
> Implicitly thy freedom staying thee! . . .

There is none of that attack on the theme that Vergil o Milton have; Crane insinuates the reader into his epic through an exclamation, "How many dawns . . .", and leaves him without a cohering centre to the perceptions until the poet himself steps forward in the third stanza, "I think of cinemas . . . And Thee . . .". "I think": if there is any theme to Crane's epic it is not the Bridge, nor America, nor the machine age; the theme is Crane himself. The Proem ends "descend And of the curveship lend a myth to God". His myth is not to be built up in a steady self-revealing pattern. It comes from something far more transitory and less definable: the *aesthetic impulse* which his Bridge or bits of American history have for him. It is always about the poet. The impulse, however, seems a very real one. Those opening stanzas have a strong inner rhythm which is unmistakably Crane's. There is clearly something happening; he is writing with all his sensibility alive to the inner disturbance. In fact, these strange inner rhythms of Crane seem to me his greatest contribution to poetry. At times they come through almost despite the sense. In the first stanza, for instance, the movement is far subtler than that declamatory moral, "Liberty", to which it leads.

Crane, in short, is something of a poetic spellbinder. His poetry imposes itself on you for all its apparent lack of discipline. Yet it does so without wooing you as the poets of the 'nineties wooed their audience, by the specious charms of stock responses. Crane's poetry is original and it moves carefully and steadily on its way, but without any clear argument. As lyric poetry, everything depends on the force of his spontaneous reactions. It demands a kind of receptive suspension. You must be sensitive to the flow of the poet's emotional response rather than to any logical train of thought. But this has, at its best, nothing to do with the unfelt rhetoric and automatic word-association which is often felt to be the outcome of the lyric impulse. Crane rarely uses inspiration as an excuse for slip-shod writing. His method may be unrational; it is not anti-rational. His best writing is guided by a purity of response which is his own equivalent of "tough reasonableness". (This applies to Crane only when he is writing well. He often wrote very badly indeed. But my object here is to see what is fresh and worth-while in his verse, not to show what everyone knows: that he had moments of inflated sentimentality which makes some of his work almost unreadable. In these places he is not at all a "great failure"; he is merely a failure.)

The queer, unreasoned element in Crane's verse has made a number of critics write of him as though he were less poetically skilful than immensely lucky; as though, beyond the initial impulse, things just happened of themselves. This is not true. The rhetorical sections of *The Bridge* apart, his method was from the start pre-eminently careful; in his most original and mature poems it was almost microscopic. Throughout his work he moved steadily in one direction. His adolescent poems are thin, but their thinness comes from too much literary tact, too much care:

> Out in the late amber afternoon,
> Confused among chrysanthemums,
> Her parasol, a pale balloon,
> Like a waiting moon, in shadow swims.
>
> Her furtive lace and misty hair
> Over the garden dial distill
> The sunlight,—then withdrawing, wear
> Again the shadows at her will.

The hesitating delicacy of movement is almost too delicate and refined. It has the thinness of an inturned aesthetic contemplation, as though the poet were in love with his own skill (you get it also in A. E. Housman). His business is with a mood which withdraws from contact; a mood controlled by words like "confused", "pale", "waiting", "shadow", "furtive", "misty", "withdrawing". For all the scene-setting and the little speech with which the poem ends, it is the opposite of dramatic. No one and nothing except the poet is involved.

Crane did not remain long with these slightly precious arabesques. By the time he was 21 the pausing aesthetic precision of his early verse was brought down to earth by a more matter-of-fact conversational tone. These two elements worked on each other to produce something more original, a sort of open-structure, translucent language:

> Walk now, and note the lover's death.
> Henceforth her memory is more
> Than yours, in cries, in ecstasies
> You cannot ever reach to share.

Up until this last stanza the poem, "Stark Major", explores the situation—the girl dead, the lover departing—in a number of rather oblique suggestions, difficult to pin down. Here the focus seems to sharpen. There is a subtle tension in the grouping of the phrases, a richness in the possibilities of which qualifies which. On one side is the meaning enforced grammatically by the punctuation, where the stress falls on "her", "yours", "you". It focuses the poem unflatteringly on the lover. And then there is the other emphasis which comes when you read with the natural pause at the end of each line. Then it is "more", "cries", "ecstasies", "ever" and "share" which take the weight. The lover is no longer so important. It is the girl who moves into the centre; her memory takes on a grandeur which is wholly out of the lover's ken. These are neither paraphrasable meanings; it is a matter of stress. But the poem has none of that blurred inadequacy Crane is often charged with. He uses the possibilities of the language to the fullest whilst remaining strictly within the limits of a slight lyric.

Certainly, "Stark Major" is no very remarkable poem. Although Crane is building on more than an evasive mood, the foundation is still slender. Perhaps it is a type of writing that any clever, accomplished amateur could, with a little luck, have done. Yet though Crane was young when he wrote this, it does not seem to me to have the usual young man's literariness. He seems too well aware of what he is about for it to be a fluke. The poem has the same sensitivity to the minutiae of language as all his maturest poems. It is a long way from the legend of Crane as the inspired but slipshod genius. The more obvious charge might be aesthetic dandyism, if it weren't that the rhythm carries the verse with considerable subtlety. It seems to have more disturbance than a mere impulse to pleasant verse-making would account for. Without that earlier, rather self-conscious hesitation, the poem has enough movement to begin to seem new and personal in a delicate, exploratory way.

But it is not fully grown poetry. Crane's most significant and original verse lies between this early, more or less aesthetic style and the coarser rhetoric of his late work. It is to be found in the poems written in about 1924 and 1925, published in *White Buildings*. They are still lyrics in the sense in which I used the term earlier: they spring from the poet's direct responses before these are mixed up with a rationalizing organization. But there is a toughening and a growing complexity in the way in which the response is realized, which is as though parallel to a highly developed intellectual complexity.

> And yet this great wink of eternity,
> Of rimless floods, unfettered leewardings,
> Samite sheeted and processioned where
> Her undinal vast belly moonward bends,
> Laughing the wrapt inflections of our love; . . .
>
> (*Voyages*, II)

There is nothing obviously lyrical about this; it is not easy, it is not even very clear. But it works in the manner of a lyric and demands the same openness and attention. This is the opening stanza; there is no main verb until the second, "Take this sea. . . ." So there is an impression—spurious, I think—that this poem follows from the end of the first of the series, "The bottom of the sea is cruel". Without a verb the action of the verse is difficult to plot; indeed, at first sight it seems to be made up only of a number of questionably connected phrases describing the sea. But seen from closer up it becomes clearer how the connections were made: how "wink" brought "rimless", which moved, with a jump, into "unfettered"; how there is a connection between the curve of the sea's eye and the curve of her "belly"; how

116

"sheeted", "belly" and "love" interact, and how the "great wink" turns into "laughing". The closer, in fact, that you look, the subtler and more deliberate becomes the interaction between the freedom and vast impersonal yearning of the sea for the moon and the limited human desires of the lovers. The progression of the poem is a series of checks and balances which work upon the reader without logical paraphernalia. Yet they work surely enough for the poet to end by drawing his morals with no great sense of strain.

I would hesitate to put a specific interpretation on the poem. It has no clear-cut meaning. It acts as a sort of mixer: it stirs up and holds together a number of related feelings about the sea and about love, but does little to separate them out. Perhaps the poetic phrase is given too absolute a value; perhaps the reader is expected to believe with too great an intensity in the uniqueness of poetic expression. Yet I don't find the atmosphere oppressive with poetic fury. There seems more to it than inflated word-association. It has a perceptive tightness of texture and a characteristic movement which could not have been wilfully imposed on a rhetorical pattern. The language, in short, does not cover up a failure in perception, nor is it, as Professor Blackmur has suggested, a perception only of linguistic qualities. On the other hand, whatever you can make of it by analysis, the method is clearly not logical. Some other way into the poem is needed.

Crane himself partly explained his way of writing in an essay which was written to accompany *White Buildings*, but not published until after his death. He talks there of "a logic of metaphor", of the "emotional dynamics of the materials used" that are "selected less for their logical (literal) significance than for their associational meanings". He then goes on to give an example from a later stanza of the poem I have just been discussing:

> When . . . I speak of "adagios of islands", the reference is to the motion of a boat moving through the islands clustered thickly, the rhythm of the motion, etc. And it seems a much more direct and creative statement than any more logical employment of words such as "coasting slowly through the islands", besides ushering in a whole world of music.

Crane is giving a truth about his method, but a partial, a self-conscious truth; the outline, not the whole story. The real point, I think, is the self-centredness of this explanation. The aura of suggestiveness of Crane's metaphors is first and foremost *subjective*. What is important is the perceiver, not the thing perceived; Crane moving through the islands, not the islands themselves; he imposes his own reactions on them. And this, of course, is precisely the lyric technique I described earlier. But instead of being allowed a whole poem to itself the lyric reaction is concentrated into a phrase or a sentence. These are like tributaries to a river, all of them are made subsidiary to the ruling impulse, the theme of the poem. The complexity of these poems, in short, lies in the fact that they are whole lyrics deepened by a number of smaller lyric impulses.

Earlier I said that Crane's subject matter was always, in one way or another, himself. This does not mean that his work has much self-dramatization in it. Nor is it dramatic in the more usual sense. In fact, he and

Stevens, for all their differences, are probably the least dramatic poets of the century. And all this is true although Crane thought he was influenced by Marlowe, although he modelled himself at times on the fashionable bits of the Jacobean dramatists and although sections of *The Bridge*, "The Tunnel" for example, are cast in a dramatic, soliloquizing form. Crane's method is less active. He once wrote that poetry of the machine age "demands . . . along with the traditional qualifications of the poet, an extraordinary capacity for surrender, at least temporarily, to the sensations of urban life." I think that all his most original poetry is made up of continual acts of surrender to sensations. But these are less often immediate physical sensations translated into words than sensations about themes, about the sea, love, death, and so on. Crane doesn't "feel his thought"; he feels instead of thinking. The instantaneous reactions of a moment are harmonized with a steady feeling for the whole theme. This is why he can seem to draw conclusions; they are not rational; they are instead his completed reaction to the subject. His poems begin with a surrender to sensations; they end with a kind of digestion of the whole subject.

Crane seems to have known very well what he was about. In most of his best poems he chose themes to suit his method; they are records of minute fractions of time so small that they begin to seem almost timeless. They are records, in short, of "this great wink of eternity", "Of a steady winking beat between Systole, diastole..." in "Paraphrase"; of the "breaking second" in "Recitative". In this last poem he sounds the theme of them all:

In alternating bells have you not heard
All hours clapped dense into a single stride?

Crane's most original work is something quite new in English or American poetry: he writes with an awareness so heightened that he makes into whole poems those sharp but transitory states from which other people's poems usually start.

I would not wish to claim too much for him. It seems only proportionate to list his weaknesses. They come mostly from the oddness of his approach. It needed a freshness and precision well-nigh impossible to maintain long. By leaning so heavily on poetic intelligence and hardly at all on common sense, Crane had very little to fall back on when his spontaneity failed. At best he trod a delicate path on the edge of rhetoric; he slipped time and again. His ambition to write great epic verse helped in this. He is invariably at his worst when his creative impulse fails to match his desire to write. The later sections of *The Bridge*, written when he was acutely aware of his failing ability, are often mawkish, rhetorical, exhibitionistic and, in places, brutal. Nearly all his long poems, in fact, are patchy. He can move effortlessly from the noisiest rhetoric to a powerful simplicity:

Spears and assemblies: black drums thrusting on—
O yelling battlements,—I, too, was liege
To rainbows currying each pulsant bone:
Surpassed the circumstance, danced out the siege!

And buzzard-circleted, screamed from the stake;
I could not pick the arrows from my side. . . .

It was Yvor Winters who first remarked that that last

line sounded like Racine. It is written with the sort of
poetic conviction which it takes genius to attain and
which makes the gesticulations around it seem all the
more unnecessary.

There are other moments when Crane does not seem
to have fully assimilated his reading:

> Whose head is swinging from the swollen strap?
> Whose body smokes along the bitten rails,
> Bursts from a smouldering bundle far behind
> In back forks of the chasms of the brain,—
> Puffs from a riven stump far out behind
> In interborough fissures of the mind . . .?
>
> ("The Tunnel")

For all the modern odds and ends—the play, for
instance, on the name of a subway system in the last
line—this seems still too firmly attached to Jacobean
dramatic verse, in a way in which the Middleton
passage in *Gerontion*, say, is not. Crane's verse has not
broken away into an independent life.

Lastly, starting with the rejection of straightforward
thinking, Crane finished too often with an approxima-
tion to what he wanted. Even when he is writing well
the rhythm of the verse is sometimes more precise and
carries more weight than the meaning of the words:

> Distinctly praise the years, whose volatile
> Blamed bleeding hands extend and thresh the height
> The imagination spans beyond despair,
> Outpacing bargain, vocable and prayer.
>
> ("For the Marriage of Faustus and Helen", III)

This is different from the excesses of Dylan Thomas's
verbalizing; Crane is not running on merely for the

sake of the words. But I feel he would have been hard put to it to explain at all precisely what he meant.

Wit, of the type found in Eliot and Pound, was never within Crane's range. Only in "Paraphrase", his finest poem, is there an ironic check on an intensely serious subject. Without that sort of intellectual defence he was left in his off-moments with shuffling exaggerations. But almost never, despite the wretched turmoil of his life, is there any self-pity in his poetry. What saved him was the gift that made his best verse, the fullness of his responses. It brought him not to self-pity but to a genuine compassion and human feeling. Perhaps this is why he saw himself, flatteringly, as an opponent of T. S. Eliot. In 1922, after the publication of *The Waste Land*, he wrote in a letter:

> There is no one writing in English who can command so much respect, to my mind, as Eliot. However, I take Eliot as a point of departure towards an almost complete reverse or direction. His pessimism is amply justified, in his own case. But I would apply as much of his erudition and technique as I can absorb and assemble towards a more positive, or (if I must put it so in a sceptical age) ecstatic goal. I feel that Eliot ignores certain spiritual events and possibilities as real and powerful now as, say, in the time of Blake. Certainly the man has dug the ground and buried hope as deep and direfully as it can ever be done. . . . After this perfection of death—nothing is possible in motion but a resurrection of some kind. . . . All I know through very much suffering and dullness . . . is that it interests me still to affirm certain things.

Crane's affirmation had nothing like the weight of Eliot's denial. His poetic talent was erratic where Eliot's was highly disciplined. He had nothing at all of Eliot's

intellectual distinction. But he did have a free and easy
emotional generosity. The workings of his poems are
minute. Yet, in contrast, his own personal reactions are
spontaneous or they are nothing. It is, I believe, this
openness and acceptance of emotions and of the facts
of the place which constitute Crane's particularly
American strength. In this he is like Whitman. The
sections of *The Bridge* called "Van Winkel" and
"The River" seem to follow fairly directly from *The
Leaves of Grass*. Crane is more sensitive to language
and far more sophisticated in his performance. But I
think his sophistication is largely of the surface. Underneath is the same inclusive bonhomie, the same strength
which is never complex and the same ability, when he
writes badly, to exaggerate and embarrass. But Crane
lived at a period when complexity seems to have been
peculiarly sought after. Partly because of the technical
revolution which was taking place in poetry, partly
because the pressures of his time and particular circumstances were more overwhelming and deadly than Whitman's, his final achievement was more difficult, more
involuted and less assured. But at his best Crane did
write from what he knew: his spontaneous and highly
individual reactions. And so his "affirmation" is not in
the great American epic, but in a handful of obscure,
powerful lyric poems. It is quite as original but altogether
slighter than he wanted.

WALLACE STEVENS

Platonic Poetry

I love work. It fascinates me. I can sit and look at it for hours.
JEROME K. JEROME, "Three Men in a Boat"

THERE has been some distinguished disagreement
about the relative excellence of Wallace Stevens's
poems and disagreement again about where
exactly the excellence lies. But there is no doubt that
excellence of a kind he had. The mere fact that Stevens
was still writing in America somehow helped preserve
the tone and standards for the rest. His assurance was
an implicit judgment on uneasy and slipshod writing.
Eliot apart, Stevens is the most perfectly finished poet
America has turned out. And this is a great deal in an
age in which so much poetic talent has been short-
circuited. Pound, Crane, Robert Lowell—to keep
only to American writers—have all produced, in their
different ways, first-class verse. Yet all are more
important in a handful of poems than in their total
œuvre. On the other hand, Stevens's achievement is
very much the sum of all his poems. Although I don't
much believe in what Marianne Moore called "the
interacting veins of life between his early and late
poems", his best poems are extraordinarily at one with
his pedestrian efforts. Stevens worked his talent to its
full. He might very easily have been a worse poet. It
is hard to see that he could have been any better. His

standard is that of accomplishment. And it is very high.

Stevens published his first book of poems in middle age—he was 44—his second big volume thirteen years later. The subsequent books appeared more frequently, but still rarely enough. When his verse first came out in bulk, that is, it was already fully formed. Indeed, most of his best known work is in that first volume, *Harmonium*. For myself, I agree with Marius Bewley: *Transport to Summer* contains poems at least as good as any in the earlier book and it has far fewer irritations of style. But though Stevens's poetry changed a little, it hardly matured. There is a new clarity to the later verse; that rather wilful ruffling of the surface has gone and it is easier to see down to the depths that are there. But maturity is a continual deepening and broadening of experience, a continually growing power of expression. Stevens's maturity is something he started with; it is a fact of middle age more than anything attained. He is intelligent and serious and mostly worth-while; but he has none of that self-renewing freshness of, say, Lawrence. Early on, Stevens seems to have discovered the theme of his poetry; he played variations on it throughout the rest of his work. Lawrence's gift was to remain continually available to experience. He lacked preconceptions where Stevens relied on them.

I have invoked Lawrence simply because of that word "maturity". Otherwise they touch at no point. If Stevens owes anything to a modern poet, it is to Eliot. He is one of the few important poets whose language was influenced by Eliot's own practice instead of by the earlier authors Eliot made fashionable. Yet whatever similarities there are—and they are few—Stevens and Eliot start from opposite directions. Eliot's poetic world is withdrawn and of a great composed formal perfection. But the stuff of it which undergoes this perfecting is the painful and changing stuff of living. Stevens's world is one of luminous and distinct images which earn their place not as they approximate to something he has gone through but as they justify ideas. The tension and pressure of Stevens's verse is all in the ideas.

He is, in fact, at a level of considerable subtlety, something of a philosophical poet; his poetry comes to rest in the clarity of abstractions rather than of experience. This section, for example, from "The Man with the Blue Guitar":

> Slowly the ivy on the stones
> Becomes the stones. Women become
>
> The cities, children become the fields
> And men in waves become the sea.
>
> It is the chord that falsifies.
> The sea returns upon the men,
>
> The fields entrap the children, brick
> Is a weed and all the flies are caught,
>
> Wingless and withered, but living alive.
> The discord merely magnifies.
>
> Deeper within the belly's dark
> Of time, time grows upon the rock.

I take it he means that the harmonies the imagination imposes—the conflicting sounds resolved in the chords of the blue guitar—are a false and blurred reality. Time perverts them all destructively and inevitably. Beneath our fictions the true and unchanging identification of things is buried, dark and threatening. Something of this order seems to be intended. What matters is that the objects he arranges in the verse resolve themselves into ideas. I'm not at all sure that the doom that hangs over it all is anything more personal than the impossibility of knowledge and the futility of art. In contrast:

> There was a man of double deed
> Sowed his garden full of seed.
> When the seed began to grow
> Twas like a garden full of snow.
> When the snow began to melt
> Twas like a ship without a belt.
> When the ship began to sail
> Twas like a bird without a tail.
> When the bird began to fly
> Twas like an eagle in the sky.
> When the sky began to roar
> Twas like a lion at the door.
> When the door began to crack
> Twas like a stick across my back.
> When my back began to smart
> Twas like a penknife in my heart.
> When my heart began to bleed
> Twas death and death and death indeed.

This is from *The Oxford Dictionary of Nursery Rhymes*. No doubt it is a good deal less polished and more wasteful than Stevens's poem. The casting around is done with less grace. But both pieces have a muffled ominousness to them; and the nursery rhyme has considerably more power. The difference is that the things are not fitted to ideas. They generate terror of themselves by a sort of perverse dream-logic. And the terror is a matter of the sharpest sensation. It is the helpless passive terror of dream suffering. The poem works to a climax of painfulness. Its logic is personal inevitability.

It seems to me that for all his care and precision Stevens never achieved this kind of inevitability. The images that bear the weight of so much of his verse seem to arrive there in a somewhat arbitrary manner.

> If there is a man white as marble
> Sits in a wood, in the greenest part,
> Brooding sounds of the images of death,
>
> So there is a man in black space
> Sits in nothing we know,
> Brooding sounds of river noises;
>
> And these images, these reverberations,
> And others, make certain how being
> Includes death and imagination. . . .
>   ("Metaphor as Degeneration")

To me, this sounds less like a poet's imagery than those eternal hypothetical tigers and rhinoceroses of the philosophers. They are chosen because they are, if nothing else, clear; there is no sense of their having chosen themselves. The logical paraphernalia that encloses them seems more important than the images themselves. In a way, Stevens was the only poet ever to take Imagism seriously. That is, he took it to its conclusion. The bulk of Imagist poetry was a more or less high-minded game played out in the consciously pregnant silences around the images. It needed an audience to be shocked into exclaiming: "How can you say so little?" and a poet who, with some satisfaction, could turn the question back on the asker: "How can you *see* so little?" But Stevens, not content with the occasionally wise passiveness the pure Imagist might, with luck, attain, made his poetry out of the problems with which those silences teemed.

What exactly the problems were has been gone over in detail a number of times. The reader had best go to the essays by R. P. Blackmur in *Language as Gesture* and by Marius Bewley in *The Complex Fate*. I will only try to give my interpretation of the theme briefly so that I can move on. It is almost a denial of Imagism, as though by practising the style Stevens had arrived at its contradiction. It is a poetry of irritation. He seems to be continually baffled by the impossibility of describing anything at all with finality. A motion of the wrist, the slightest variation in light or in the mood of the observer, and the object is utterly different. The impossible endlessness of observation, then, is Stevens's creative premiss. Almost any of his ambitious poems will have this theme hidden away in it somewhere; to give just three examples of three quite distinct manners: "Metaphors of a Magnifico", "Sea Surface Full of Clouds" and "The Man With the Blue Guitar". Perhaps the studied manner in which he has varied his rhetoric is an attempt to evolve an instrument flexible enough to cope with his subject. I will return to this. The acceptance of limitation, however, is only a beginning. The better the verse, the more strenuously he works towards something more positive. Things as they are are at their best a little frustrating, at their worst deadening and negative. But there is, he discovers, a moment at which they come truly alive: the moment at which they are caught in all their subtlety by the imagination. Then they take to themselves meaning. And this is not a projection of the poet's self. It is a moment of purity when what is grasped is neither the commotion at the surface of the thing observed nor the commotion inside the observer. It is something that sparks between them: an essential imaginative life. As a procedure it sounds almost unexceptionable, so long as it remains a demand for rigorous disinterestedness. It doesn't.

> You must become an ignorant man again
> And see the sun again with an ignorant eye
> And see it clearly in the idea of it.
>
> Never suppose an inventing mind as source
> Of this idea nor for that mind compose
> A voluminous master folded in his fire.
>
> How clean the sun when seen in its idea,
> Washed in the remotest cleanliness of a heaven
> That has expelled us and our images . . .
>
> ("Notes Toward a Supreme Fiction", I)

Stevens at his best—and this has all the superb conviction of his best—is not merely acting on poetic principle, on something that will give him the best practical results; he is involved in a tense logical process which takes him from the purity of the description to the idea of the thing described. He has come out on the far side of Imagism into its opposite, the Platonic world of Ideas.

Of course, there is no clear-cut ontology in Stevens's poetry, no world of meaning that has its separate

existence aside from the poetry, like the "meaning" of
Spenser's allegory—whatever that is. Stevens's style
is too rooted in images for generalizations ever to get
away in it on their own. But his preoccupations take
him off into a realm where his poetry must get along
on a rarified diet. It is a question of what the poet feels
strongly about. And Stevens has great feeling for two
things: for the truth that lurks below the changing
surface of appearances, and for the mode by which this
is perceived, the imagination. Certainly, the truth
Stevens's imagination seizes upon is kept supple and
varied by its dealings with images; but its method
of dealing with them is more questionable. In his
Princeton lecture he was quite firm about the business
of the poet:

> . . . although he himself has witnessed, during the long period
> of his life, a general transition to reality, his own measure
> as a poet, in spite of all the passions of all the lovers of truth,
> is the measure of his power to abstract himself, and to with-
> draw with him, into his abstraction, the reality on which the
> lovers of truth insist. He must be able to abstract himself, and
> also to abstract reality, which he does by placing it in his
> imagination.

I am suspicious of such high-mindedness. But the
extraordinary thing is the pertinacity with which
Stevens stuck to his beliefs. A poet's penchant for
theory as often as not makes little difference to his best
poems; Coleridge's, for instance. But in Stevens's work
it is all important; not only are his poems again and
again about themselves, about the imagination, about
the validity of metaphor, and so on; underneath all his

work is an abiding *belief* in abstraction. His poetic method is controlled by an abstracting principle. Unless you are willing to treat his imagery only as a set of toy bricks, carefully made and elegantly arranged, you find yourself forced away continually into a spare, abstract world. For example, a large number of his poems have the titles of paintings—"Woman Looking at a Vase of Flowers", or "The Well Dressed Man With a Beard"—yet the titles are on a mere nodding acquaintance with what follows. It is often as though he had left out the opening stanzas from his poems. The reason is that for Stevens a scene, an object, is only a starting-point for a voyage into abstraction. His method is the exact reverse of the slogan William Carlos Williams uses in his epic *Paterson*: instead of Williams' axiom, "No ideas but in things", Stevens has "No things but in ideas". The ideas are interpretative of the images; they are not rigid and separate generalizations. His "Examination of the Hero in Time of War", for instance, has nothing whatever to do with the concept of the hero, but everything to do with the modes by which we, the observers, apprehend the hero. It seems as though Stevens was never happy unless he could have all the images and figures with which his verse abounds tidied away into a framework of decent abstraction. His poetry is analytical—away from the detail towards the related ideas. I am convinced that his favourite word is "it". He is, anyway, the great poet of the third person. However much he may conceive of the imagination as an instrument of profound insight, he uses it to arrive at the type of coherence that a philosopher is more usually intent on. Stevens's, in fact, is the reverse of the usual method of poetry which starts out with the fullness of the experience, worries away at the hidden motives, and leaves the abstractions to take care of themselves. Perhaps it is this insistence on reasons and his relative indifference to motives that gives that air of arbitrariness to much of Stevens's imagery. For his images don't have to define; they are instead the source of definitions.

Stevens is a philosophical poet only in a specifically modern manner: he believes in the need for coherence and perhaps would like to arrive at some sort of finality, if it were not that he hardly trusts even philosophy itself. It is as though he had read the subject at Oxford. So he ties his deductions to observation, and proceeds steadily, minutely, without any unjustifiable spurts from generalizations and with few conclusions large enough to notice. Instead, he seems intent on making the best of a bad philosophical world. His air is at times foreboding, almost grim, as though only he really knew quite how bad things are, and how important are the least clearings of sense he can make. There is a certain hopeless poignancy in his persistence in the hunt for what he feels all along to be ultimately elusive.

However many and obscure the regions into which he follows his quarry, he is always stalking the same creature: imaginative coherence. And he always ends with the same painful sense of what might have been. It is this that, for me, makes many of his long poems almost unreadable: they are difficult, very difficult, but below the trouble is a certain steady repetition; you work down to what he is saying on *this* topic only to find that it is much the same as he has always said about

everything else. It is like a number of very elaborate
dwellings carved into the same cliff-face. Everything he
has to say is in his two masterpieces, "Sunday Morning"
and "Notes Toward a Supreme Fiction". The first is his
profoundest statement of disbelief in anything beyond
what is now; the other is his final tribute to the imagination, the power which justifies and dignifies his disbelief.
This last catching together of all the themes in his work
shows how deeply he feels them, how important the
abstractions are for him. This is not always apparent
elsewhere. Often his abstractions can rouse him to no
more than stylistic device; and then the repetition is not
solely in the theme:

> Inescapable romance, inescapable choice
> Of dreams, disillusion as the last illusion,
> Reality as a thing seen by the mind,
>
> Not that which is but that which is apprehended,
> A mirror, a lake of reflections in a room,
> A glassy ocean lying at the door,
>
> A great town hanging pendent in a shade,
> An enormous nation happy in a style,
> Everything as unreal as real can be,
>
> In the inexquisite eye . . .
> ("An Ordinary Evening in New Haven", V)

The air is logical, but the effect is of a number of rough
drafts for one statement, as though the randomness
were trying to lose itself in multiplication. There is a
point with Stevens, and he reaches it often, at which
profundity becomes blurred with rhetoric.

His rhetoric is at times **a distra**ction from what he is
saying, at others it is the **whole tale**. Stevens's fatal

Cleopatra was undoubtedly the turn of phrase. I find it difficult to know quite how to take his encrusted style. Certainly, in much of the earlier verse there is a large element of game; but the dandyism continues where game is seemingly not in question:

> If men at forty will be painting lakes
> The ephemeral blues must merge for them in one,
> The basic slate, the universal hue.
> There is a substance in us that prevails.
> But in our amours amorists discern
> Such fluctuations that their scrivening
> Is breathless to attend each quirky turn.
>
> ("Le Monocle de Mon Oncle," VI)

The rhetoric seems to build up a motion of its own, not quite that of the poem's start. I feel Stevens had not decided whether to be compelling, ironical, or merely whimsical. And yet his extraordinary rhythmical control, that sense of perfect balance and strictness without ever using, or needing, rhymes, is an assurance at least that the hesitation is not in the craftsmanship. It is a matter, I think, of the medium itself. Throughout his work, and particularly in *Harmonium*, Stevens seems to me to be writing in a language that does not quite belong to him. It has something of the quality of the latinized English of the seventeenth-century scholars; it is done with skill, precision and devotion, but the writer is never quite able to get the sound of older, foreign voices out of his own. Often it is something more tenuous and a good deal more subtle than rhetoric:

> If her horny feet protrude, they come
> To show how cold she is, and dumb.
>
> ("The Emperor of Ice-Cream")

It is a beautiful and solemn cadence. But behind it somewhere, and I am not sure how far behind, is the echo of another poet. I can be no more precise than that. Since I first read the poem a long time ago, I have been trying to remember what it reminds me of. But without success. R. P. Blackmur suggested that Stevens's early rhetoric has affinities with Marlowe. It seems to me much closer to that of Sir Thomas Browne: quiet and intelligent, concerned only with one or two problems which come up again and again, beautifully embellished in a language full of the echoes of earlier stylists.

Stevens's style, of course, is in no way imitative; but it is something contrived. Often there is a disparity between his elaborate furnishings and the rather stringent bareness of the ideas. And even in those poems where meaning and style go most together he still moves, and is moved, by indirections:

> Above the forest of the parakeets,
> A parakeet of parakeets prevails,
> A pip of life amid a mort of tails.
>
> (The rudiments of tropics are around,
> Aloe of ivory, pear of rusty rind.)
> His lids are white because his eyes are blind.
>
> He is not paradise of parakeets,
> Of his gold ether, golden alguazil,
> Except because he broods there and is still.
>
> ("The Bird with the Coppery, Keen Claws")

For all the incisive delicacy and wit, there is some sort of deliberate redundance in the writing. He proceeds like a fashionable hostess at someone else's party; at each step he pauses for an elaborate gesture: "Aloe of ivory, pear of rusty rind", "Of his gold ether, golden alguazil". No doubt part of the wit lies in the exotic style; here the grandiose exaggeration is very much to the point. But often the gestures claim all of your attention—the over-rated "Bantams in Pine-Woods", for example—and then the poems hardly exist below the level of style.

The poems that have received too little attention are a number of far quieter ones, in which the style is subdued into clarity, and the lack of surface commotion leaves the metrical perfection to speak for itself. I am thinking of pieces like "The Snow Man", "The Curtains in the House of the Metaphysician", "Gubbinal", "Two at Norfolk", "Restatement of Romance", "Château Gallant", "Less and Less Human, O Savage Spirit", "The House Was Quiet and the World Was Calm", "The Beginning". There are a large number of these—poems of the order of Robert Frost's best, "Never Again Would Bird-Song Be the Same"— and they show how very accomplished Stevens was. It was the consistency of his output that somehow, as I said at the start, seemed to preserve the standards of good writing. And yet the absence in these poems both of the dominant themes and the hard surface of stylistic device makes me feel that Stevens did not set very much store by them. They seem to have happened a little to one side of his main creative effort. Yet the qualities he set most by—sustained precision of movement and sustained richness of style—which at other times puff his poetry up, as though with ambition, in these poems relax into a slighter and more personal perfection.

137

Perhaps the word "ambition" is the key to all the hesitations I have about Stevens's poetry. He is content to let these smaller poems go with personal statements. But his bigger themes are entangled with his theory of abstraction and a purity of perception which has only disdainful truck with the personal world. In the poems in which Stevens more or less succeeds with his ideal—there are many of them, and they are beautiful and original—the writing has an extraordinary lucidity; it was not for nothing that his ideal of perfection, as Mr Bewley pointed out, was in the word "transparency". But when he failed to attain this perfection, he was left only with the means to it: a principle of continuous abstraction and a certain elegance of expression. Left hanging in the air without personal support, these seem sometimes a little pathetic, sometimes trivial.

Stevens was too intelligent and too gifted to be content with small subjects. His grand purpose was serious, lucid and difficult. Twice he achieved it, in "Sunday Morning" and "Notes Toward a Supreme Fiction", and these are great poems; a number of times he got very near it, in, for example, "Le Monocle de Mon Oncle", "Peter Quince at the Clavier", "The Idea of Order at Key West"; he also wrote a number of excellent and much slighter poems. But in his ambitious failures— "An Ordinary Evening in New Haven", for example, or "The Comedian as the Letter C"—he leaves you only with the precision and elaboration of method and ideas. Personally, I don't share his enthusiasm for these. And so I find the poems dull. It may be a little late to begin to quibble with words, but there is one hair that

needs to be split: at some time while Stevens was discovering what he had to say about the world, he became
muddled in the distinction between poetic *intellect* and
poetic *intelligence*, The first he always has—hence the
rigour and tight-lipped skill of his verse. The other,
like most other poets, he can only fully achieve from
time to time.

D. H. LAWRENCE

The Single State of Man

Art itself doesn't interest me, only the spiritual content.
D. H. Lawrence, Letter to Eunice Tietjens, 1917.

THE only native English poet of any importance to survive the First World War was D. H.
Lawrence.[1] Yet his verse is very little read. As
a minor adjunct to the novels it has come in, on occasions, for a little off-hand comment. More often it is
used as a go-between, joining the prose to the biography.
Anthologists have printed a few poems grudgingly, out
of piety, and even the critic who introduced the best
English selection, in *The Penguin Poets*, seemed to feel
that the poems succeed despite themselves, because
they were written by Lawrence.

I had better state my position straight away: I think
the poems very fine indeed, with a fineness of perception
and development that was always Lawrence's, and an
originality that makes them as important as any poetry
of our time. For their excellence comes from something

---

[1] Robert Graves, whose poetry I admire, does not seem to me to have
survived the war. For all his debonairness he has remained essentially a war
poet. That is, he has created a drawing-room art out of anything but
drawing-room feelings. His moments of savagery and tenderness appear like
crevasses in a snowfield, unexpected and disconcerting. Lawrence himself
summed it up in *Aaron's Rod:* "In this officer, of course, there was a lightness
and an appearance of bright diffidence and humour. But underneath it was
all the same as in the common men of all combatant nations: the hot, seared
burn of unbearable experience, which did not heal nor cool, and whose
irritation was not to be relieved. The experience gradually cooled on top:
but only with a surface crust. The soul did not heal, did not recover."

that is rare at best, and now, in the 1950s, well-nigh lost: a complete truth to feeling. Lawrence is the foremost emotional realist of the century. He wrote too much verse, like Hardy and Whitman, the two poets who influenced him most. But even his badness is the badness of genius; and there are quite enough good poems to make up for it. As for the influences and the styles he brushed with, Georgian and Imagist, I will have nothing to say of them here. They have no part in his best work.

Lawrence's poetry is usually hustled out of court by way of its "carelessness". I believe it was Eliot who first said that Lawrence wrote only sketches for poems, nothing ever quite finished. In one way there is some truth to this: he was not interested in surface polish; his verse is informal in the conventional sense. Indeed, the tighter the form the more the poet struggles:

> Many roses in the wind
> Are tapping at the window-sash.
> A hawk is in the sky; his wings
> Slowly begin to plash.   ("Love Storm")

It is the last word that jars. I see what he means, but the need to rhyme is like a wedge driven between the object and the word. The thing is forced and uneasy, even a little journalistic. Again and again, when Lawrence uses strict metrical forms, the poetry fails because of them, or succeeds despite them. At times he can manage complicated stanzas, but only because they allow him to get away from close correspondence of rhyme; they give him space to move around. The fainter the chime, the more remote the echo, the more convinced the poetry seems; close and perfect rhyme is invariably a constriction to him. For an essential part of Lawrence's genius was his fluency; and I mean something more literal than the ease with which he wrote: rather, the sense of direction in all the flowing change and variation in his work. This fluency has its own forms without its own conventions. It is not plottable: ear-count, finger-count and what might be called the logic of received form have nothing to do with it. What matters is the disturbance. "It doesn't depend on the ear, particularly," he once wrote, "but on the sensitive soul." It is something that can never be laid out into a system, for it comes instead from the poet's rigorous but open alertness. And so there is care, even discipline, but no formal perfection and finish. In an introductory note to *Fire and Other Poems* Frieda Lawrence wrote: "He just wrote down his verse as it came to him. But later, when he thought of putting them into a book to be printed, he would work them over with great care and infinite patience." And she has remarked that in a way he worked harder at his poetry than at the novels. When the prose would not go right he threw it away and began afresh. But the poems he worked over again and again. As proof there are the early drafts of "Bavarian Gentians" and "The Ship of Death", which are now printed as an appendix to the *Collected Poems*. Still, his diligence had nothing to do with mere technical efficiency. Lawrence's controlling standard was delicacy: a constant, fluid awareness, nearer the checks of intimate talk than those of regular prosody. His poetry is not the outcome of rules and formal craftsmanship, but of a purer, more native and immediate artistic sensibility. It is poetry because it could not be otherwise.

He was well aware of what he was about. He put his case in the introduction to *New Poems*:

> To break the lovely form of metrical verse, and dish up the fragments as a new substance, called *vers libre*, this is what most of the free-versifiers accomplish. They do not know that free verse has its own *nature*, that it is neither star nor pearl, but instantaneous like plasm. . . . It has no finish. It has no satisfying stability, satisfying for those who like the immutable. None of this. It is the instant; the quick.

If Lawrence is trying to get the weight of formalism off his back, it is not for laziness. "The instant; the quick" is as difficult to catch, to fix in exact language, as the most measured and stable formulations of experience. For this sort of impulse is in opposition to poetic conventions. The writer can never rely on a code of poetic manners to do part of the work for him. At the same time, of course, Lawrence knew his own powers and limitations well enough to realize that "art" in some way deflected him from the real poetry. "Art for my sake", he said. Perhaps this is what he meant in the introduction to the *Collected Poems*:

> The first poems I ever wrote, if poems they were, was when I was nineteen: now twenty-three years ago. I remember perfectly the Sunday afternoon when I perpetrated those first two pieces: "To Guelder Roses" and "To Campions"; in springtime, of course, and, as I say, in my twentieth year. Any young lady might have written them and been pleased with them; as I was pleased with them. But it was after that, when I was twenty, that my real demon would now and then get hold of me and shake more real poems out of me,

making me uneasy. I never "liked" my real poems as I liked "To Guelder Roses". . . . Some of the earliest poems are a good deal rewritten. They were struggling to say something which it takes a man twenty years to be able to say. . . . A young man is afraid of his demon and puts his hand over the demon's mouth sometimes and speaks for him. And the things the young man says are very rarely poetry. So I have tried to let the demon say his say, and to remove the passages where the young man intruded. So that, in the first volume, many poems are changed, some entirely rewritten, recast. But usually this is only because the poem started out to be something which it didn't quite achieve, because the young man interfered with his demon.

This is at the opposite pole to Eliot's defence of Pound's hard work. For Eliot, the continued business of versifying was a way of keeping the bed aired until such time as the Muse should decide to visit. Lawrence's work was in coming to terms with his demon, so that the utterance would be unhindered. For it was the utterance, what he had to say, which was poetic; not the analysable form and technique. So for all his trouble, he never innovated in Pound's or Eliot's way. His discoveries were a matter of personal judgment and response. In the poems the speed and stress varies with the immediate, inward pressure. This is why the words "loose" and "careless" so clearly do not describe Lawrence's verse.

To have an example down on the page, there is "End of Another Home Holiday". To my mind, it is the best of the early *Rhyming Poems*. The demon has his say without awkwardness, but there is just enough of the earlier contrivance to show what Lawrence had left behind:

D. H. LAWRENCE

When shall I see the half-moon sink again
Behind the black sycamore at the end of the garden?
When will the scent of the dim white phlox
Creep up the wall to me, and in at my open window?

Why is it, the long, slow stroke of the midnight bell
    (Will it never finish the twelve?)
Falls again and again on my heart with a heavy reproach?

The moon-mist is over the village, out of the mist speaks the bell,
And all the little roofs of the village bow low, pitiful,
    beseeching, resigned.
—Speak, you my home! what is it I don't do well?

Ah home, suddenly I love you
As I hear the sharp clean trot of a pony down the road,
Succeeding sharp little sounds dropping into silence
Clear upon the long-drawn hoarseness of a train across the valley.

  ·   ·   ·   ·   ·   ·   ·   ·   ·   ·

The light has gone out from under my mother's door.
    That she should love me so!—
    She, so lonely, greying now!
    And I leaving her,
    Bent on my pursuits!

      Love is the great Asker.
      The sun and the rain do not ask the secret
      Of the time when the grain struggles down in the dark.
      The moon walks her lonely way without anguish,
      Because no-one grieves over her departure.

Forever, ever by my shoulder pitiful love will linger,
Crouching as the little houses crouch under the mist when I turn.
Forever, out of the mist, the church lifts up a reproachful finger,
Pointing my eyes in wretched defiance where love hides her
    face to mourn.

Oh! but the rain creeps down to wet the grain
That struggles alone in the dark,
And asking nothing, patiently steals back again!
The moon sets forth o' nights
To walk the lonely, dusky heights
Serenely, with steps unswerving;
Pursued by no sigh of bereavement,
No tears of love unnerving
Her constant tread:
While ever at my side,
Frail and sad, with grey, bowed head,
The beggar-woman, the yearning-eyed
Inexorable love goes lagging.

The wild young heifer, glancing distraught,
With a strange new knocking of life at her side
  Runs seeking a loneliness.
The little grain draws down the earth, to hide.
Nay, even the slumberous egg, as it labours under the shell
  Patiently to divide and self-divide,
Asks to be hidden, and wishes nothing to tell.

But when I draw the scanty cloak of silence over my eyes
Piteous love comes peering under the hood;
Touches the clasp with trembling fingers, and tries
To put her ear to the painful sob of my blood;
While her tears soak through to my breast,
  Where they burn and cauterise.

   .   .   .   .

The moon lies back and reddens.
In the valley a corncrake calls
  Monotonously,
With a plaintive, unalterable voice, that deadens
  My confident activity;

D. H. LAWRENCE

> With a hoarse, insistent request that falls
>   Unweariedly, unweariedly,
> Asking something more of me,
>   Yet more of me.

I have put the poem there in full because, like all of
Lawrence's verse, it needs its whole length to express
its complexity. It seems to me a difficult poem. Yet
there is nothing immediately incomprehensible about
it, none of those tough intellectual obstacles that stop
you short in Eliot's work. There is a curious intermix-
ing of people and scene and nature. But beyond that
the difficulty is in the state of mind: the pull between
love and guilt, the tension between man and child.

It is all in the first four lines. They have a kind of
awakened rhythm which cuts below the expectations of
formality to the "sensitive soul". As Lawrence said of a
line by Whitman, "It makes me prick my innermost
ear". Only in the first ten-syllabled line will finger-
count pay. After that the poem moves off on its own
way. There is more in question than nostalgia: the
speed of the lines varies with the flexibility of the talking
voice. Part troubled, part meditative, the nostalgia is
quickened instead of being expanded into a mood. If
my comments are vague and assertive, I can only add
another assertion: they have to be. Everything depends
on the reader's direct response to the rhythm. In that
is all the disturbance which the rest of the poem defines.

Perhaps "define" is the wrong word; "draw out"
might be closer. For what follows is done without a
hint of abstraction. What is there to be defined is a
complex of feelings, nothing that can be tidily separated
out into formulae. All that is possible, and all the poet

attempts, is to reach through intelligence some balance in the conflict.

> Why is it, the long, slow stroke of the midnight bell
> (Will it never finish the twelve?)
> Falls again and again on my heart with a heavy reproach?

There are three forces: the young man, literary and fond of word-painting; then, undercutting him, uneasy impatience; and finally, guilt. Mercifully, there is no need to go through the poem line by line to show how these two feelings take over all the details of the scene, so that it becomes a sort of living presence for the poet to face. The result is that he can move from his village to his mother, from natural to artistic creation, without the least strain.

The poet is peculiarly unembarrassed and open about his feelings. He values his independence, but he doesn't assert it: the hint of self-absorption in "Bent on my pursuits" has the same touch of irony about it as, for example,

> But when I draw the scanty cloak of silence over my eyes
> Piteous love comes peering under the hood;

And his central theme, "Love is the great Asker", is both acknowledgment *and* criticism: the demands of love touch the vital part of him, "Where they burn and cauterize"; yet even while they expose what is shallow and selfish in him, they expose themselves by their own nagging insistence.

The theme is love, but there is nothing in the poem of a "Definition of Love", with all that implies of dapper logic and clear-cut distinctions. Lawrence's

148

logic is more intimate. It is carried forward by a rigorous worrying, probing down to the quick of the feelings.
Although the personal conflict is set off by the cycle of
nature, no parallels are drawn. The forces work in
harmony rather than in contradistinction. Despite all
the talk of the sun and the moon, the grain and the
heifer, and even that "slumberous egg", the focus
stays personal. In phrases like

> No tears of love *unnerving*
> Her constant tread

you see how the same difficult, intimate preoccupation
runs under the whole thing. So without any of Marvell's
syllogizing there is still a completeness to the poem;
in the end, something has been settled. It is done by
what Eliot called a "logic of sensibility" (though, in
fact, he probably meant something quite different).
The toughness, instead of being in the logic, is in the
truth to feeling, the constant exertion of the poet's
intelligence to get close to what he really feels, not to
accept on the way any easy formulation or avoidance.

This is why a set metre would have been impossible
—as it was impossible in Coleridge's "Dejection".
Each line has its own force and rhythm, and they flow
together, varying with the shifts in feeling. This is
true of almost all Lawrence's poems; the inner pressure
and disturbance gives to every one its own inherent
form. Each starts afresh and appeals directly to the
attention of "the sensitive soul". The controlling factor
is in the intelligence. His poems are not effusions;
they don't run off with him. Instead, the intelligence
works away at the emotions, giving to each poem a

finished quality, an economy in all the repetitions. It is a matter of the fullness with which the subject is presented.

This intelligent honesty and pertinacity of Lawrence's verse has had very little attention. The poems which have come in for most notice, the *Birds, Beasts and Flowers*, are usually thought of as little more than vivid little pieces of description, like the so-called "lyric" passages in his novels. In fact, the nature poems are quite as personal as any of his others. In them he doesn't merely describe, nor does he go at his subjects with a preconceived idea and try to twist them into meanings they would not naturally take. They are neither all subject nor all poet. It is a matter of a vital and complex relationship between the two, difficult, fluent, inward and wholly unabstract. He even avoids the final abstraction of formal perfection. For that gives to experience a kind of ghostly Platonic idealness: in the end, everything is so perfectly accounted for that the poetic world is complete and isolated. In the relationship Lawrence tries to catch, everything is in flux; it is a flow between two creatures, with nothing fixed. The artist has constantly to improvise at the full pitch of his intelligence. And according to Lawrence, who judged intelligence by its delicacy and awareness, not by its command of rationalization, the greater the intelligence the nearer the result came to poetry:

> It has always seemed to me that a real thought, a single thought, not an argument, can only exist easily in verse, or in some poetic form. There is a didactic element about prose thoughts which makes them repellent, slightly bullying.
>
> (Foreword to *Pansies*).

The same sort of intelligence is at work in the novels, but the actual method is rather different. Again, the didactic sections hardly matter—though in some of the later novels they take up more space than they are worth. The whole method is to set the characters in motion, so there is a curious fusion of feeling and action, each dependent on the other, deepening the other, and yet resisting any single interpretation. Hence the word "symbolism" that is often tacked on to his method; I prefer Dr Leavis's term, "dramatic poem". Of course, Lawrence himself is there in all his novels; but at the remove of fiction. There is no need to make an exact identification, for the author has given himself enough room to dramatize and judge with a free hand. The poems are more intimate, and their personal statements are outright. He said of the *Collected Poems*: "I have tried to establish a chronological order, because many of the poems are so personal that, in their fragmentary fashion, they make up a biography of an emotional and inner life". There precisely is the difference: the theme of both the novels and the poems is fulfilment, the spiritual maturity achieved between man and woman. But in the novels the fulfilment is acted out; the forces, like the morality, are "passionate, implicit". By contrast, the poems present nakedly the inner flow that runs below the actions, the forces before they are externalized in drama. It is as though they presented not the body that acts but the blood itself, the lifeline of experience and feeling that feeds and supports the novels.

Here, for example, is a passage from a novel which develops much the same theme as "End of Another Home Holiday":

No man was beyond woman. But in his one quality of ultimate maker and breaker, he was womanless. Harriet denied this, bitterly. She wanted to share, to join in, not to be left out lonely. He looked at her in distress, and did not answer. It is a knot that can never be untied; it can only, like a navel string, be broken or cut.

For the moment, however, he said nothing. But Somers knew from his dreams what she was feeling: his dreams of a woman, a woman he loved, something like Harriet, something like his mother, and yet unlike either, a woman sullen and obstinate against him, repudiating him. Bitter the woman was grieved beyond words, grieved till her face was swollen and puffy and almost mad or imbecile, because she had loved him so much, and now she must see him betray her love. That was how the dream woman put it: he had betrayed her great love, and she must go down desolate into an everlasting hell, denied, and denying him absolutely in return, a sullen, awful soul. The face reminded him of Harriet, and of his mother, and of his sister, and of girls he had known when he was younger—strange glimpses of all of them, each glimpse excluding the last. And at the same time in the terrible face some of the look of that bloated face of a madwoman which hung over Jane Eyre in the night in Mr Rochester's house.

The Somers of the dream was terribly upset. He cried tears from his very bowels, and laid his hand on the woman's arm saying:

"But I love you. Don't you *believe* in me? Don't you *believe* in me?" But the woman, she seemed almost old now—only shed a few bitter tears, bitter as vitriol, from her distorted face, and bitterly, hideously turned away, dragging her arm from the touch of his fingers; turned, as it seemed to the dream-Somers, away to the sullen and dreary, everlasting hell of repudiation.

He woke at this, and listened to the thunder of the sea with horror. With horror. Two women in his life he had loved down to the quick of life and death: his mother and Harriet. And the woman in the dream was so awfully his mother, risen from the dead, and at the same time Harriet, as it were, departing from this life, that he stared at the night-paleness between the window-curtains in horror.

"They neither of them believed in me", he said to himself. Still in the spell of the dream, he put it into the past tense, though Harriet lay sleeping in the next bed. He could not get over it.

This is from *Kangaroo*, where Somers is no less Lawrence than the much younger man who wrote the poem. And the same demon is at work in both, the same crucifixion between guilt and love, between independent male activity and unanswerable emotional ties; and, in the end, the same sense of inevitable betrayal. Yet although the dream allows Lawrence to use a kind of emotional shorthand and a bare directness of presentation, the novel and the poem only converge from opposite directions. In the verse the feelings *are happening* to the poet in all their conflict. In the novel they are embodied in action. They are given sides and the complexity is left to flower in the spaces between.

The whole of Lawrence's power and originality as a poet depends on the way he keeps close to his feelings. This is why he had to rid himself of conventional forms. The poems take even their shape from the feelings. And so it is a long way off the mark to think of them as jotted-down talk. The span of the lines is not that of the talking voice. The tone is: that is, it is direct and without self-consciousness. But the poems, for instance, use more repetitions than talk. Yet this is a matter of fullness, not of rhetorical elaboration. It is part of the purposefulness with which the poems explore the emotions in their entirety. And with the same sureness he can let them go; when he is writing from no more than an impulse or an irritation, short and transient, the poetry is equally brief and to the point—*Pansies*, for example; but when the feelings are profound and sustained, so is the verse-form: as in, say, "Bavarian Gentians", one of his masterpieces. The dependence of the form on the subject means that the poems find it very hard to rarify themselves into mere words and device.

The lines themselves help to the accuracy and delicacy of the expression. They are a means of emphasis rather than a pause for breath:

He drank enough
And lifted his head, dreamily, as one who has drunken,
And flickered his tongue like a forked night on the air, so black,
Seeming to lick his lips,
And looked around like a god, unseeing, into the air, . . .

("Snake")

Again, it is a question of movement, or rather of two movements, one playing against the other. There are actions, the ordinary, recognizable sanity of things happening in a human, or almost human way; these get the short matter-of-fact lines: "He drank enough", "Seeming to lick his lips". And then, in subtle contrast, is the running, disturbed movement of the longer lines in which the poet catches up the factual description into his own excitement. The known merges with the unknown: "as one who had drunken" becomes "like a forked night on the air", and ends "like a god". And so, within the framework of a description, the interchange between these two creatures takes on the dignity of a strange visitation. He is unloosing, in fact, the reserves of power of two earlier lines in the poem:

> Someone was before me at my water-trough,
> And I, like a second comer, waiting.

For all the implications, there is nothing "otherworldly" about this. The stuff of Lawrence's poetry, the "lifeline", are those essential experiences in which he registers his full humanity. His poems are the inner flow of a man in the act of becoming aware—aware not only of his feelings and their cause, but of their full implications. By the flexibility of his verse-forms he can catch this flow in all its immediacy, and with peculiarly little fuss. For fuss has no part in what he has to say. Lawrence is not a mystic; his poetry has to do with recognitions, not with revelations. It should be read not against the cant of "dark gods" and the stridency of *The Plumed Serpent*, but against the sanity of the "creed" with which he answered Benjamin Franklin:

> That I am I.
> That my soul is a dark forest.
> That my known self will never be more than a little clearing in the forest.
> That gods, strange gods, come forth from the forest into the clearing of my known self, and then go back.
> That I must have the courage to let them come and go.
> That I will never let mankind put anything over me, but that I will always try to recognize and submit to the gods in me and the gods in other men and women.

There is only reverence, attention, awareness and an unprejudiced independent intelligence at the bottom of this; no other-worldliness, nothing in the least of overblown pretension. It is the imaginative strength with which Lawrence voiced the fullness of his humanity that has got him the name of mystic and prophet, as it did for Blake. Lawrence does not have second sight, he has only a piercingly clear first sight. His genius is in rendering that, rather than waiting until his perceptions have gathered about them a decent abstraction, as the warm-blooded body of a whale is enclosed in protective blubber. Lawrence's mysticism is merely his first-handness, his distance from convention.

Earlier, I remarked that the controlling force in the verse is neither any formal metrical guide nor a set of preordained principles; it is the working intelligence. On this his most genuine and effective poetry relies. The intelligence is primarily in the honesty with which he acknowledges his feelings and recognizes his motives with neither shuffling nor abstraction. But it is there too in the wit, the endless liveliness of his verse:

> How beastly the bourgeois is
> especially the male of the species—
>
> Presentable, eminently presentable—
> shall I make you a present of him?

Or

> It is a fearful thing to fall into the hands of the living God
> But it is a much more fearful thing to fall out of them. . .

Or

> You tell me I am wrong.
> Who are you, who is anybody to tell me I am wrong?
> I am not wrong.

D. H. LAWRENCE

The closeness of this last to "For Godsake hold your tongue, and let me love" seems to me to be apparent enough. Yet Lawrence's verse, for all its wit and swing, has never been resurrected in the craze for Donne. The reason is simply that the twentieth-century Metaphysical style has been used as an excuse for obliqueness. The canons of irony invoked to display its excellence are merely ways of avoiding commitment, a technical sleight of mind by which the poet can seem to take many sides while settling, in fact, for none. Lawrence, clearly, does not suffer from this—neither, I believe, did Donne. The wit of both is not a sparkle on top of indifference; it is a manifestation of intelligence:

> Imagine that any mind ever *thought* a red geranium!
> As if the redness of a red geranium could be anything but a
> sensual experience
> and as if sensual experience could take place before there
> were any senses.
> We know that even God could not imagine the redness of a
> red geranium
> nor the smell of mignonette
> when geraniums were not, and mignonette neither.
> And even when they were, even God would have to have
> a nose to smell at the mignonette.
> You can't imagine the Holy Ghost sniffing at cherry-pie
> heliotrope.
> Or the Most High, during the coal age, cudgelling his mighty
> brains
> even if he had any brains: straining his mighty mind
> to think, among the moss and mud of lizards and mastodons
> to think out, in the abstract, when all was twilit green and
> muddy:

"Now there shall be tum-tiddly-um, and tum-tiddly-um,
hey presto! scarlet geranium!"

We know it couldn't be done.
But imagine, among the mud and the mastodons
god sighing and yearning with tremendous creative yearning,
        in that dark green mess
oh, for some other beauty, some other beauty
that blossomed at last, red geranium, and mignonette.

It is hard to know whether to emphasize more the ease
and originality of the piece, or its tact. There is neither
a jot of pretentiousness in the poem, nor of vulgarity,
though the opportunity for both certainly offered.
Lawrence uses his wit not in the modern fashion, to
save his face, but to strengthen the seriousness of what
he has to say. There is no disproportion between the
colloquial liveliness of the opening and the equally
alive tenderness of the close. The wit is not a flourish;
it is one of the poetic means; it preserves the seriousness
from sentimentality and overstatement, as the seriousness keeps the wit from flippancy.

Lawrence wrote too many poems. Their standard is
not uniformly high; some of them are frankly bad. In
this count I am leaving out *Pansies* and *Nettles*. Though
some of these are good, they were intended primarily as
squibs; and even if they have a serious enough edge to
their satire, few are particularly memorable as poetry.
Nor is he to be held responsible for the faults of his early
verse; they are the faults of a poet who is still trying to
find his own voice. The bad poems are those which have
a complete originality, yet still fail. For example, the
sequence "Wedlock" in *Look! We Have Come Through!*
the transitional volume. Like his best poems, they go

down to the pith of the feelings and present that in its singleness. But they fail because they are too naked. It is as though the feelings were overwhelming beyond speech, yet still the poet insisted on nothing less than their full force, muffled by no sort of poetic device. In "Burnt Norton" Eliot justifies a long series of images which suggest an intense experience without stating it, by the comment: "Human kind Cannot bear very much reality". In these poems, Lawrence is insisting on nothing short of the emotional reality, and the poetry cannot quite bear it. They are not private as the *Pisan Cantos* are private; they have no references which remain in the poet's keeping. They are private in the other sense: they make the reader feel he is listening in where he shouldn't be. It is for this reason that *Look!*, although it contains some excellent poems, is more successful as a series than in any one piece. Lawrence himself said, "They are intended as an essential story, or history, or confession", and Amy Lowell thought they made up "a greater novel even than *Sons and Lovers*". That is an overstatement which was worth making. The impact of the book seems to me as direct and painful as anything since Clare. Yet it would be hard to localize this power in any one poem. If some of the pieces fail because of their nakedness, it is because they are approaching the vanishing-point of poetry, where expression itself is some sort of intrusion. It took genius and great courage even to fail in that way. When Lawrence's poems are bad they are victims of that peculiar honesty which, at other times, made for their strength.

Lawrence was honest about the emotions without

being absorbed in them for their own sakes. He is not taken up in himself. The life-line of his poems is something more active, harder and more delicate. "But it's no good", he wrote to Murry, "Either you go on wheeling a wheelbarrow and lecturing at Cambridge and going softer and softer inside, or you make a hard fight with yourself, pull yourself up, harden yourself, throw your feelings down the drain and face the world as a fighter.—You won't though". Lawrence's poems are about that "hard fight". He never relished his feelings, nor played with them in front of the mirror; hence he never simplified them. But he always kept extraordinarily close to them; and so he never fell into oversubtlety, the intellectual counterpart of emotional looseness. The language· of the poems, lucid, witty, vivid, often a bit slangy, preserved the balance. It made any kind of overstatement or evasion very hard.

The question why Lawrence's poetry has had so little recognition, despite its originality, delicacy, wit and, above all, its honesty and intelligence, is answered in that word "carelessness". Our modern poetry began with a vigorous attack on outworn conventions of feeling and expression. But the emphasis has gradually gone so much on the craft and technicality of writing that the original wholeness and freshness is again lost. One sort of academic nullity has been replaced by another: the English "gentleman-of-letters" conceit, which prevailed at least until the end of the Georgians, has gone under. In its place is a Germanic *ponderismuskeit*, a deadening technical thoroughness. Lawrence's demon is as out of place in that as it was in the old port-and-tweed tradition.

D. H. LAWRENCE

I used to think that one of the troubles with the poetry we have now was that, despite the stress Eliot has laid on the intelligence, no one seemed capable of thinking. I was wrong—not about the inability to think, but in expecting it at all; or at least in expecting thinking to be carried on with something of the precision of the seventeenth century. Of course, no one is trained in the syllogism; nowadays that sort of logical clarity is impossible, or it is forced. In place of the old patterns the modern poet has to rely far more heavily on his own native intelligence, on his ability to feel accurately, without conceit or indulgence; to feel, that is, when he has "thrown his feelings down the drain". He is left then not with a vague blur of emotions or a precise, empty dialectic, but with the essential thread that runs beneath the confusion, with "the instant; the quick". This, I believe, is the real material of poetry, material which could not take any other form. This inner logic is quite as difficult as its older formal counterpart. It depends on getting close to the real feelings and presenting them without formulae and without avoidance, in all their newness, disturbance and ugliness. If a poet does that he will not find himself writing in Lawrence's style; but, like Lawrence, he may speak out in his own voice, single and undisguised.[1]

---

[1] Since writing this chapter it has occurred to me that the clue to the technical originality of Lawrence's mature verse may be that it has a different metrical norm from most other English poetry. Its point of departure is not the iambic pentameter; instead, it is the terser movement of his narrative *prose*. I can see no other way of explaining the extraordinarily wide and subtle variation of rhythmical period within the span of a single line of free verse.

ART AND ISOLATION

Indeed, we are but shadows; we are not endowed with real
life, and all that seems most real about us is but the thinnest
substance of a dream—till the heart be touched. That touch
creates us—then we begin to be—thereby we are beings of
reality and inheritors of eternity.
HAWTHORNE, "Note-Books"

I

THERE is one quality shared by nearly all modern
poets: difficulty. And by "modern" I mean
poetry which began to be written towards the
close of the First World War and was, in fact, most
obviously "modern" thirty or more years ago. None of
the work was difficult simply because it was experimental, or because it dealt with fresh and unexpected
materials. Every new movement seems, in this way,
strange and stiff to its original audience; the readers
are awkward with it, as though hearing a new language.
But that wears off. It is an accidental quality, whilst, for
the modern poets, difficulty was a means. Not that it
was an end in itself. Eliot claimed that our poetry was
difficult because it had to be; that is, because it was the
product of a difficult and complex civilization which,
"ethics having been eclipsed by psychology", had
become impressively aware of its own complexity. No
doubt Eliot was right; but there were also other reasons
nearer home. Above all, the two prime movers in
modern poetry, Eliot and Pound, were both American
by origin. Perhaps, then, part of the difficulty of modern
poetry had to do with its Americanism: it was attempt-

162

ing to express a kind of insight which had at best been sketchily suggested in poetry and given its full weight only in a very few novels. They were not insights in the European tradition; hence the iconoclasm of the modern poets and the deliberate way in which Eliot and Pound set about rebuilding the tradition to suit themselves. What is difficult in modern poetry is not its references, its intricate syntax, but its tentative, exploratory independence from all traditions. It gives, in Melville's words, "the impression, that whatever swift, rushing thing I stood on was not so much bound to any haven ahead, as rushing from all havens astern".

English poetry has often been very difficult indeed. At its best it has always that complexity of attitude which Dr Leavis would call the mark of its "maturity". But that difficulty is part of the nature of poetry; it is in the writer's effort to bring to bear all the weight of his experience and intelligence on whatever he is talking about. The full suggestiveness of his work relies on a kind of creative response from the reader, whose relationship with the poet is an intimate one, based on a certain gratitude and a certain respect. For they begin with the same world of values. The only essential difficulties are those of the reader's emotional education. It is only very rarely—with some of Blake, for example, or less of Crashaw—that the ground between the poet and his readers is shadowy and hard to map. However far most other poets travel, they have their readers with them when they begin. On the other hand, really obscure poets may cut across or even end in country the readers know; but where they begin is remote.

Obscurity, then, is not a question of technique but

of the amount of common ground between the poet and his audience. Provided they agree that even the most sensitive and original experience can be discussed, and that discussion of it is an important and valuable activity, then, no matter how strange and original the poetry may be, it will never finally be obscure. For the writer will have a basic ease and freedom with the moral world from which his work is created.

This fundamental courtesy has often been denied American writers, despite all the other spectacular courtesies at present lavished upon them. So there is in much of the best American work a suggestion of tenseness, which seems at times almost something physical, like a stutter. It makes at times for their great originality; and it always gives the impression of considerable effort in the teeth of what the poets can and cannot take for granted. I suggested in the chapters on Pound and Eliot that Americans coming to poetry at the beginning of this century had almost nothing to go on, not even a properly substantiated poetic language from which to develop and differ. Compared with the novel, American poetry hardly existed. So the poets found themselves quarrelling with the English tradition— which was a healthy quarrel, but not quite to the point. The great effort of Pound and Eliot was not merely to inject life into an art which had faded into one of spent, harmonious truisms, but to do so by writing English with the strengths of foreign languages. Perhaps in this way they managed to evolve a language adequate to the complex sensibility of our time. But they also managed to evolve a new formal mode: an American poetic language. Hence Pound writes English as though he had just invented it, whilst Eliot, in his peculiarly subtle modern way, has created a poetry which, however near the norm of spoken language it begins, is the most formal since Milton set about writing a Latin epic in English. Not that their writing has lost anything in purity or power by this. On the contrary; both have used the genius of the English language to its full. But to do so both have had on occasions powerful foreign models and have used them to insist on the sheer difficulty of writing anything at all. Eliot, for instance, says of the passage in "Little Gidding" which I have discussed: "One of the most interesting things I learnt in trying to imitate Dante in English, was the extreme difficulty. This section of the poem —not the length of one canto of the *Divine Comedy*— cost me far more time and trouble and vexation than any passage of the same length that I have ever written." I think this section of the poem is the finest thing Eliot has ever done; but it is typical of the great strictness of his creative effort that excellence and difficulty should be directly proportional to each other. In the same way, at the beginning of their maturity, he and Pound found some of their strength with the help of the elaborately chaste craftsmanship of Gautier.

Of course, I cannot prove that this preoccupation with creating a fresh, difficult language for poetry was specifically American. But as a suggestion it fits with what happened on both sides of the Atlantic. The work of Eliot and Pound was only part of a great experimental movement in the States; they may have encouraged it, but it began and continued independently of them. Moreover, Eliot's example has in fact done some-

thing to crystallize out the language of American poetry:
Stevens's "Notes Toward a Supreme Fiction", one
of the most important poems to come out of America,
would not have had that tough, translucent purity
unless the poet had had before him the example of the
Four Quartets. And then none of the important English
writers, neither Yeats, nor Lawrence, nor Graves, nor
Auden, have anything like the same, formal, difficult,
experimental air. They are all altogether more off-hand.
Even with Dylan Thomas the only difficulty, I find,
comes from my reluctance to believe that such simple,
enthusiastic feelings need so many complicated words
to express them. But then I confess I do not really
understand the tradition of Welsh pulpit oratory. Perhaps a feeling for that would go a long way towards a
taste for Thomas. As it is, there seems to me to be an
awesome gap between the performance of the poet
himself reading his own poems, and the poems printed
there on the page. Hearing Thomas perform, there is
no doubt that this is the authentic thing, the real sense
of poetry. Yet though the poems in cold print have at
times a sense of power, often a sense of groping magnificence, they have most often one of somewhat overbearing verbal preciosity. Perhaps Thomas's genius for
poetry was second to his personal genius; his verse was
above all part of his aura, something he carried around
with him, like his Elizabethan face. Even among his admirers the poetry seems not quite as important as the
myth of the poet. His obscurity may be an effective part
of the myth, part of the stubborn belief that genius is
always out of our ken; but it is not, I think, inherent in
the material with which he copes.

ART AND ISOLATION

I am not suggesting that English poetry of the twentieth century has been any easier to write or that it has expressed anything less subtle and inclusive than American work. The difference is that the English poets have had to worry less about their basic values and their audience; about, in short, their literary manners.

Ever since James wrote his essay on Hawthorne, American critics have been debating the question of the manners of art. Recently it was revived in two important essays by Lionel Trilling: "Manners, Morals, and the Novel" and "Art and Fortune". In its details, the debate is concerned with the novel, but its implications touch upon all American art. Briefly, Trilling accused American society of lacking sufficient "social texture" to support the true novel:

> The characteristic work of the novel is to record the illusion that snobbery generates and to try to penetrate to the truth which, as the novel assumes, lies hidden beneath all false appearances. Money, snobbery, the ideal of status, these become in themselves the objects of fantasy, the supports of the fantasies of love, freedom, charm, power. . . .

In Europe the undemocratic stratification of society allows a rich interplay between classes, each of which has, relatively, its own distinct culture. In the States, on the other hand, the class structure is fluid; there may be social distinctions, but they are not final—that powerful American optimism could hardly exist if they were. Consequently, there is little strength in unvoiced values, in what Trilling calls "a culture's hum and buzz of implication"—that is, its manners. The effect, Trilling thinks, has been somehow to debilitate the American novel:

> I think that if American novels of the past, whatever their merits of intensity and beauty, have given us very few substantial or memorable people, this is because one of the things which makes for substantiality of character in the novel is precisely the notation of manners, that is to say, of class traits modified by personality. . . . All great characters exist in part by reason of the ideas they represent. The great characters of American fiction, such, say, as Captain Ahab and Natty Bumppo, tend to be mythic because of the rare fineness and abstractness of the ideas they represent; and their very freedom from class gives them a large and glowing generality; for what I have called *substantiality* is not the only quality that makes a character great. They are few in number and special in kind; and American fiction has nothing to show like the huge, swarming, substantial population of the European novel, the substantiality of which is precisely a product of a class existence.

I think Trilling is both right and wrong: right in his analysis of the difference between European and American art; wrong in believing that the American writer is necessarily crippled by the difference. He is only in difficulties when he encroaches on ground where "manners" are necessarily in command. But much of his power and strangeness comes from the fact that he does this so rarely; the focus of American art is different from ours. But I will return to this later.

"A culture's hum and buzz of implication" is more difficult to analyse in poetry than it is in the novel. Poetic manners have little or nothing to do with any preoccupation with technique—which is at present an American fad—and very little to do even with the over-nice correctness of Eliot's early Jamesian poems. Perhaps the only modern American poet who really is concerned with manners is Robert Frost, although his are never as complex as those whose absence Trilling laments. Yet I think this is why Frost has been so readily accepted in England; he is peculiarly congenial; we are easy with the tradition of country poetry, simple language and simple wisdom. American cosmopolitan-ism, even Eliot's, has always appeared a suspicious virtue, whereas Frost seems assured, he does not have to strive; he has New England behind him.

This is partially true. We do know the tradition, and Frost is apart from most other American verse. He has a known formal easiness on which his reputation has been firmly established on both sides of the Atlantic. Indeed, his New England admirers seem nostalgically to assert that Frost *is* the American tradition; the rest is aberration. But there is an underlying difficulty with Frost's poetry; that is, to recognize how much of the tradition he merely took over and how much he had to make up for himself.

Reading through a collection of his works, it is strange how Frost's poems sound almost familiar; Crabbe, Hardy, Edward Thomas, even Clare, worked in the same area. The poems are almost familiar, but not quite. There is a certain toughness to Frost that is not the same as Crabbe's moral firmness. There is also a certain monotony that I find hard to define. I would call it the monotony of literary effort.

The toughness is not puzzling. It goes with the kind

of poetry Frost writes. For he is not a nature poet; his work has none of that personal interpretative weight. He is a country poet, whose business is to live with nature rather than through it. His desire is to formulate, to make not merely the best but the clearest of his experience; not to present experience in all its fullness, as, at their best, Hardy or Edward Thomas did, but to draw a moral. Hence Frost rarely leaves the conclusions to take care of themselves; instead, he continually coaxes the reader the way he wants him to go. Not that he is heavy or obvious with his directives. It is a question of emphasis. For example, his poem on "The Sound of Trees":

> They are that that talks of going
> But never gets away;
> And that talks no less for knowing,
> As it grows wiser and older,
> That now it means to stay.

The first two lines make one of those beautiful and vivid perceptions on which Frost's reputation rests securely. It is what follows, particularly the fourth line, that jars. There is a refusal to let be, a refusal to allow the reader to do a little of the creative work for himself. Frost's insistence on his meaning is to poetry what the over-use of italics is to prose—more of an irritation than a help. It gives the impression that he is trying to drum into an unresponsive audience how moving and profound the small things of life can be. In this he is not unlike William Carlos Williams, who also constantly admonishes his city readers to use their eyes for their greater pleasure and edification. But Williams, though less polished, manages to say his say without that touch of condescension.

The result, in Frost's less distinguished verse, is an uneasy air of premeditation. His generalizations, instead of coming the hard way, have about them a touch of simplification, at times almost of glibness. Of course, he is dealing with a realm in which simplicity is correct. But the faint uneasiness is there because in many of the earlier poems the means to simplification are not unaffected and rustic, but literary and self-conscious. It is extraordinary how much "poetical" language is lying around in the first volumes, despite the fact that his themes and essential style have changed very little in his whole career as a poet. Granted Frost began to write a very long time ago, so his archaisms are probably not all deliberate; and granted his singleness of colloquial tone must have needed great practice and hard work to perfect. Nevertheless, the literariness is a surprising contrast both to his habitual air of plain wisdom and to the lucidity he reaches in his best work. For then he assumes without hesitation all those stresses of his particular time and place which Trilling would call the "manners". Frost's real achievement is, in fact, in this intimate assumption of a tone: a peculiarly subtle ease in his language and a complete economy of statement.

But only by reading through his collected poems do you realize how he has worked for this ease. If his best poems seem just to happen, he has arrived at this spontaneity only by endless disciplined effort. The original, utterly natural cadence of

> Admittedly an eloquence so soft
> Could only have had influence on birds . . .

is founded on practice in long-winded colloquial monotony:

> He fell at Gettysburg or Fredericksburg,
> I ought to know—it makes a difference which:
> Fredericksburg wasn't Gettysburg, of course.
> But what I'm getting to is how forsaken
> A little cottage this has always seemed . . .

If the rhythm is dead, that is because the colloquial pattern is as wilfully applied and as carefully worked over as any insistent traditional metre. Indeed, a number of Frost's short poems and, with the exception of "A Servant to Servants", "West-running Brook" and "The Witch of Coös", all his poetic anecdotes are valuable chiefly as experiments in handling colloquial rhythms and in refining his language to its essentials, as he refines his experience in order to draw conclusions from it.

It is a difficult process. For simplicity in poetry is attained, at the best, only rarely. It comes not from ignoring discordant elements but from writing with a clarity and delicacy which will include and go beyond them. The great master of the style is George Herbert; and even a poem as well known as "Love bade me welcome" shows how his purity is founded on a kind of social tact. Frost, too, has achieved simplicity, but sporadically and as a wit, rarely in his more direct moral poems. For in those he pares so much away that what he finally presents sometimes seems a little crude. For example, there is the beautifully simple

> Yet for them the lilac renewed its leaf,
> And the aged elm, though touched with fire;
> And the dry pump flung up an awkward arm;
> And the fence post carried a strand of wire.

For them there was really nothing sad.
But though they rejoiced in the nest they kept,
One had to be versed in country things
Not to believe the phoebes wept.

where the description takes so naturally the poet's
rather fragile sadness that the interpretation seems to
take on the actual lineaments of the things described.
Yet within a few pages he can produce an equally
characteristic poem, which ends like an Americanized
and up-ended "Pippa's Song":

Leaves got up in a coil and hissed,
Blindly struck at my knee and missed.
Something sinister in the tone
Told me my secret must be known:
Word I was in the house alone
Somehow must have gotten abroad,
Word I was in my life alone,
Word I had no one left but God.

His tone is not usually as portentous as this, but Frost
does at times put more strain on his simplicity than it
can easily bear.

His effort towards simplicity, in fact, has two directions: one presumes literary manners, the other laments
them. The lamentation is always implicit; it is a matter
of an unyielding reduction of his material until he has
reached a basic morality of depression:

No memory of having starred
Atones for later disregard,
Or keeps the end from being hard.

Better to go down dignified
With boughten friendship at your side
Than none at all. Provide, provide!

There is no doubt about the power of this. And Frost has a number of similarly bleak successes—"Acquainted with the Night" is another particularly good one. The command of rhythm and of off-hand language combine to make these poems seem as though they were founded on a hard-bitten, everyday wisdom. Yet their real power comes from their moral remoteness, from their utter denial that any positive qualities can ever be assumed without fighting for them.

This is Frost as the New England sage, formulating his sparse working morality. There is also a poet of wit in Frost, whose master is not Crabbe or Hardy but Herrick, the writer who used country things for his own sly purposes. And as it did with Herrick, the slyness at times gets the better of him; Frost the wit falls into overdeliciousness and is whimsical. On these occasions he lacks Herrick's relish and assurance; he is the Puritan putting on Cavalier airs. What he calls "the old sweet-cynical strain" fails, when it does fail, by forcing the gay, worldly-wise tone. Either, in the later political poems, the jauntiness rings hollowly, or the point seems hardly worth making:

> The rain to the wind said,
> "You push and I'll pelt."
> They so smote the garden bed
> That the flowers actually knelt,
> And lay lodged—though not dead.
> I know how the flowers felt.

I could wish that Frost were not, on occasions, quite so appealing. But where his debonair style succeeds—in, say, "Never Again Would Birds' Song be the Same",

or "The Silken Tent", or many of the short poems in
A Witness Tree and *New Hampshire*—something perfect in its naturalness, flexibility and perception has
been achieved.

They are perfect, but they haven't very much weight.
I would hardly say they have behind them the massive
support of the New England tradition, which is
reputed to be something sterner and more conscience-
ridden. Instead, they are founded on *an idea* of what
New England should represent—a kind of cultured
simplicity. No doubt Frost did not have to invent this
idea, but he certainly had to create the poetic style with
which to express it. There is throughout his work the
mark of an extraordinary literary effort by which he
has adapted more or less traditional English forms to
every colloquial modulation of his own voice. The con-
sequent grass-roots sophistication has every mark of
being a personal creation: the result of his fine technical
control and great will-power. It has nothing essentially
to do with New England's "hum and buzz of implication". Instead, Frost has managed to coax New
Englanders into accepting his interpretation of them.

III

Perhaps I am twisting the word "manners" in a way
that Trilling would not wish to credit. Perhaps, too,
it will appear outdated to take up an argument that has
been debated up and down for so long—particularly
one which was based on James's criticism of Hawthorne's America. The situation is very different now.
The contemporary American poet is better off than any
artist has been since the decay of patronage. The

Universities employ him to teach "creative writing", he receives fellowships from vast and princely founda-tions, magazines pay him startlingly and the publishers of high-minded paper-backs make his work easily accessible to a large audience. So before he is out of his twenties he is, as like as not, settled into his own neat little house, with an ice-box as large as Verlaine's garret. Yet when John W. Aldridge recently renewed the debate on manners in his book *In Search of Heresy*, it was precisely these rewards that he attacked as somehow cheating the artist of his real satisfactions:

> The writer is . . . placed in the most paradoxical of situa-tions. Through the reprint market he gains access to an immense potential audience but never to an effective, articulate public. If his sales are at all typical, he achieves through that market the financial status of the established, successful writer but not the reputation, or the means of reputation, by which such status must be accompanied if it is ever to be real. He consequently finds himself with his medium impoverished to the point where the only sense he has of his literary existence is that abstractly provided him by his sales reports and royalty checks.

As Aldridge sees it, the modern methods of mass-distribution, by their very efficiency, have made the States larger and more indeterminate than ever. The writer's success itself has assimilated him into a parti-cularly anonymous class: he is neither very rich, nor, relatively, is he a poor outsider; he is respectable, a member of the comfortable bourgeoisie, like a host of other well-paid technicians. He has been made, in fact, into a literary technician, who teaches creative writing as a craft like any other. It is hardly surprising that

Aldridge takes the short step from criticizing the vast indifference of the American audience to agreeing with Trilling's strictures on the thinness of American social texture.

Yet, in all respects for both these critics, I cannot see that these conditions are wholly debilitating. There are a number of great artists who have survived the disadvantage of not being Western Europeans: Dostoievsky, for example. The University poets in the States may be depressingly self-conscious and contriving; but University poets nearly always are. The really creative minds have produced a kind of art which may be utterly different from that of Europe, but it is no less effective or less profound for that.

The difference is one of primary assumptions. The first fact that has always faced the American writer is precisely, I think, the blankness and indifference of his audience. Hawthorne felt it; so did Thoreau and James; so did Eliot when he wrote his essay on James; it is at the root of Hart Crane's obscurity. I imagine that it is not far removed from the strange, untouched, inhuman remoteness of the landscape itself, as it must have faced the Americans less than a century ago, and as it still is in the West. It is this assumption of a fundamental isolation that makes for the peculiar strength of the American intellectual and the American artist.

I do not want to overdramatize the scene. I am merely trying to suggest a reason for the insistent, often belligerent individuality of the American writers. In his introduction to the *Faber Book of Modern American Verse*, Auden pointed out the extraordinary technical difference between the major modern poets in the

States; he thinks it is based on the belief that "it is up to each individual poet to justify his existence by offering a unique product". It may be, but there is also a more fundamental dissatisfaction behind this yearning to begin afresh. Few original American intellectuals and artists have been able to give themselves with much conviction to democratic conformity; and so each, if he wants a moral world complex enough to satisfy him, must in some manner build it up for himself. This, at least, is my impression. In the States it is very easy to assume what an intelligent man does *not* believe in; the reverse is equally difficult.

This is particularly true of the intellectuals. They can, in fact, hardly be said to build up their moralities at all; they reach them by a process of sceptical reduction. They seem to judge less from what they believe in than from what they are not taken in by. In all their enthusiasms, they are responsible finally to an abiding core of scepticism, of common sense. Someone has suggested that this is what is left of the Puritan's insistence on individual conscience. Perhaps; but that particularly deep-rooted scepticism seems to me more Jewish than Puritan; that is, much more an individual's instinct for sanity and survival than a principle or tradition. It is something inherited from the faults of society rather than from its strengths. It is this kind of minimal sanity on which the best and least pretentious verse of William Carlos Williams and Winfield Townley Scott is built. As poetry it is not very profound, but it is occasionally impressive as a statement of the American negative virtues.

The major creative artists, however, need something

more than the negative virtue of scepticism for their starting point. "It is", said Lawrence, "the pure disinterested craving of the human male to make something wonderful, out of his own head and his own self, and his own soul's faith and delight, which starts everything going." Yet the American artist begins with the fact of his isolation from conventional values and a certain indifference in his material, like the blankness of a stone wall. Trilling and Aldridge conclude that because of this blankness the characters a novelist creates cannot declare themselves through the richness of their setting; instead of dwelling in the realm where "moral realism" has its home—that is, the delicate realm of social interaction—they must involve themselves exclusively in the world of action. The novelist, in fact, finds himself always committed to telling a tale if he wishes to avoid a kind of rapt conceit in the isolation of his sensibility.

If the great American novels are no more than immensely compelling adventure stories, they have none of the usual characteristics of the genre, none of that Q.E.D. structure which leads to a triumphant happily-ever-after. Instead, they are peculiarly inconclusive. Moby Dick is not killed; Huck Finn just "lights out for the territory"; no one is given a medal in *The Red Badge of Courage*; even Holden Caulfield, in *The Catcher in the Rye*, is left only with the dubious assistance of psycho-analysis. As tales they hardly justify themselves.

If a great novel like *Moby Dick* has affinities with any other kind of literature it is with the heroic. That is, the action, however obscurely, is for a purpose. The earliest heroes were proving themselves worthy of kingship; they were the saviours and preservers of the tribe, the redeemers of the waste land. The American hero, in his isolation, is not concerned with this. He is responsible to himself. Not, I insist, to his selfishness, but to his own world of knowledge and values and feelings. Aldridge quotes Morton Zabel as saying: "It is (the hero's) passion for a moral identity of his own that provides the nexus of values in a world which has reverted to anarchy". The hero's passion begins to show itself in action, for this puts to test all the primary qualities: courage, pity, generosity, integrity. And these are qualities which come of isolation and nakedness rather than of social give-and-take. Of course, if they were all that was emphasized, the novels would be nothing more than a glorification of the cult of manliness—which they are not. But from this foundation the writer moves inwards in a strange, tentative, probing way, as though, in the middle of all the turbulence, he expected to come face to face with himself. Melville interpreted Shakespeare in this way:

> It is those deep, far-away things in him; those occasional flashings-forth of intuitive Truth in him; those short, quick probings at the very axis of reality,—these are the things that make Shakespeare, Shakespeare. Through the mouths of the dark characters of Hamlet, Timon, Lear, and Iago, he craftily says, or sometimes insinuates, the things which we feel to be so terrifically true that it were all but madness for any good man, in his proper character, to utter, or even hint of them. Tormented into desperation, Lear, the frantic king, tears off the mask, and speaks the same madness of vital truth. But, as I said before, it is the least part of genius that attracts admiration.

And so, much of the blind, unbridled admiration that has been heaped upon Shakespeare has been lavished upon the least part of him. And few of his endless commentators and critics seem to have remembered, or even perceived, that the immediate products of a great mind are not so great as that undeveloped and sometimes undevelopable yet dimly discernable greatness to which those immediate products are but the infallible indices.

It is a profoundly original comment on Shakespeare, particularly for that date. But it is an equally profound comment on Melville's own work. *Moby Dick*, for instance, is really sea-like in the way in which you can never focus on any firm surface, even of action. There is a shimmer of other meaning over everything, as though Melville's whole purpose were to bring into substantial being a whole world of intuited, half-known truths. In fact, all his work is guided by this creative effort to get at an abiding core of inner knowledge. The hero of his masterpiece, *Bartleby*, is not only "the naked, unaccommodated man"; he has, by his eternal "I prefer not to", acted to its conclusion the moral and theological problems of free-will and self-responsibility. Almost everything Melville wrote has about it that sense of swarming potentiality which is the surest mark of the poetic imagination.

If Melville is typical of the most original American artists, then the better and more powerful their work the nearer it draws to poetry. And this has nothing to do with technique with words; Melville's intended poeticisms seem to me little more than an awkward Elizabethan journalese. What matters is that the artist views his material without the intricate filters of social convention. In fact, he hardly *views* it at all; he feels it nakedly, as though every scene and event were part of his inner life. By virtue of the qualities which have been counted his drawbacks—his isolation and the bareness of his moral world—the American artist can at times attain an extraordinary inwardness. For through the relative economy of the tale he is dealing with the intense, hidden fears and exactitudes of a man creating his own world and discovering his own values. It is this queer inwardness, where nothing is ever quite finished but the sense of what is possible grows all the time, that makes for the power and originality of the great American novels and tales. It has nothing to do with introspection; it is an ability to put into moving substantial form the artist's own moral tensions.

IV

No American writer has had a poetic imagination as profound as Melville's, but the best of them have the same kind of difficulty. *Ash Wednesday* in this respect is not at all American. It is a very difficult poem indeed; it presents the inner process of spiritual preparation with a subtle and complete economy. Yet in doing so it presumes on a prior order, that of religious orthodoxy. Hence the impersonal formality seems not at all at odds with the intimacy of the experience. The specifically American difficulty comes from the poet's inability to rely on any steadying framework outside himself.

The poetry of Richard Eberhart, for example, is continually plagued by a great lust for a system. He seems to find abstractions unbearably appealing; but only, I think, because they are by way of being a reassurance. The real force of his poetry has nothing to do with abstractions. He writes as though in protest against sharp and painfully baffling feelings. His language has a kind of physical complexity which makes him sound as though he had been surprised into it almost unwillingly. When he writes:

> Oh where
> Has gone that madness wild? Where stays
> The abrupt essence and the final shield?

the difficulty is peculiarly unintellectual. It lies in his attempt to fix in words an obstinate physical desire for the metaphysical. I cannot believe in Eberhart's Blakean mysticism, though he has otherwise been influenced by Blake in a particularly creative way: he has found with Blake's help a way of dealing with the most recalcitrant material. But Eberhart's mysticism, like his metaphysics, is theoretical. Instead, the poet has a genius for expressing directly feelings far too complex and powerful to explain. And so he seems to believe that the absolute qualities are, as it were, owed to him. Such metaphysical system as he has does not exist at all in its own right; he attains it by a process of induction from his own disturbance. In his best poems there are no abstractions which are not given body by his peculiar immediacy of expression:

> You would think the fury of aerial bombardment
> Would rouse God to relent; the infinite spaces
> Are still silent. He looks on shock-pried faces.
> History, even, does not know what is meant.

You would feel that after so many centuries
God would give man to repent; yet he can kill
As Cain could, but with multitudinous will,
No farther advanced than in his ancient furies.

Was man made stupid to see his own stupidity?
Is God by definition indifferent, beyond us all?
Is the eternal truth man's fighting souls
Wherein the Beast ravens in its own avidity?

Of Van Wettering I speak, and Averill,
Names on a list, whose faces I do not recall
But they are gone to early death, who late in school
Distinguished the belt feed lever from the belt holding pawl.

The achievement is to make of a sense of shock so profound that it becomes a criticism of God, a wholly unpretentious statement of a pitying, dignified. but undistinguished humanity. That awkwardness, which is typical of his best verse, does not come because Eberhart cannot manage anything more polished. Rather, it is a way of emphasizing the isolation of his statements: they presume on no prior means and no accepted manners. The awkwardness is a product of the man himself, as though his sharply original intuitions came almost against his will, accompanied by the enthusiastic embarrassment of the conventional American in him. Yet this adds to the power. Eberhart's rhetorical mysticism is poor and his deliberate literary effects, even his similes, are never particularly convincing. In contrast, his way of suddenly juxtaposing unexpected words does not have about it any hint of device. It seems an effort, made in all honesty, to force into common daylight sensations he can only gropingly apprehend.

ART AND ISOLATION

Richard Eberhart and Robert Lowell are the two most impressive American poets since the generation which flourished in the 'twenties. They have in common almost nothing except this powerful, shut-in awkwardness. In Lowell's poetry there is a deliberate wooing of ugliness. Since he has great skill and control over his medium, I presume the chopped-up lines and broken rhythms are precisely what he is after:

> In the sperm-whale's slick
> I see the Quakers drown and hear their cry:
> "If God himself had not been on our side,
> If God himself had not been on our side,
> When the Atlantic rose against us, why,
> Then it had swallowed us up quick."

The last line jerks back from the rhetoric as violently as if the poet had burned his fingers on it. And this is typical of the movement of Lowell's poetry. It goes with the clotted, difficult texture. My impression is that he wishes to avoid every point of rest which order and formality might give. His language is wonderfully rich in its suggestions, but everything is directed towards a state of the most acute dis-ease. If Lowell does at times have a rhetoric—and I think he has—it is one of ugliness. Marius Bewley has written brilliantly and in detail on Lowell in *The Complex Fate*. He defines the tortured, harsh quality of his poetry as the result of "a head-on collision between the Catholic tradition and an Apocalyptic Protestant sensibility". I can't argue with that, but would add that clearly neither force wins. That is why the work is so difficult. Despite the determinedly Catholic symbolism, a final *balance* in the stability of the Church is not even attempted. The poetry reflects the private conflicts painfully and honestly enough. But it doesn't offer anything very certain beyond that. It is as though, although he continually returns to it, Catholicism were to one side of the real work. Lowell's essential poetry is in the unresolved private turmoil.

Both Eberhart and Lowell have worked with considerable power to make of their obscure emotional disturbances a matter of more general and deliberate truth. Elsewhere this creative effort has been turned, neatly enough, into a technique for dispensing sometimes striking, sometimes merely flashy effects. There is, for example, the poetry of Theodore Roethke. Roethke has a far more slender talent than Eberhart or Lowell, but a talent of a kind he most certainly has. When he published *The Lost Son* in 1948 he was managing to deal with his private troubles both directly and with real delicacy:

> This urge, wrestle, resurrection of dry sticks,
> Cut stems struggling to put down feet,
> What saint strained so much,
> Rose on such lopped limbs to a new life?
>
> I can hear, underground, that sucking and sobbing,
> In my veins, in my bones I feel it,—
> The small waters seeping upward,
> The tight grains parting at last.
> When sprouts break out,
> Slippery as fish,
> I quail, lean to beginnings, sheath-wet.

The poem, which is called "Cuttings", has its occasion

and its subtlety of reference; it would be hard to say where exactly the buds and the private yearnings blend into each other. Since Roethke's confessions never embarrassed him, they never had that overbearing, claustrophobic intensity of confessional poetry; instead, the work had a very immediate purity.

Unfortunately, in the volume which followed, *Praise to the End!*, Roethke was no longer serving his material he was exploiting it:

> A deep dish. Lumps in it.
> I can't taste my mother.
> Hoo. I know the spoon.
> Sit in my mouth.
>
> A sneeze can't sleep.
> Diddle we care
> Couldly.
>
>> Went down cellar,
>> Talked to a faucet;
>> The drippy water
>> Had nothing to say. . . .

And soon it reads as though some amateur psychologist had given him a pat explanation of the earlier poems, and from then on the poet had used his verse as though it were the analyst's couch. There is an air of coy exhibitionism to it all. Roethke has since turned to a more staid, Yeatsian movement which, like even his worst poetry, has moments of vivid sensation. But he has succumbed to the same temptation that has also been the downfall of the contemporary American novelist, Saul Bellow: that is, he regards his nervous intensity and upset as somehow a mark of his difference and glory. It is this that sets the artist apart from the comfortable bourgeois surroundings in which his success has landed him. His artistic identity becomes a matter of his refusal to conform placidly. He ends where the important writers begin, in that sense of isolation from which they create an impersonal artistic order: "In dreams begin responsibilities."

v

I have been trying to suggest no more than one difference between English and American poetry. And it is a difference which is strong only in the best American work, for it is a matter of the way in which the creative energy forces itself into the material; which means there must from the start be considerable energy present. By creative energy I mean a power more subtle, intelligent and impersonal than, say, the witty but bumptious individualism of Delmore Schwartz or the emotional banality e. e. cummings has disguised beneath his energetic virtuosity with a typewriter. I mean instead the way artistic imagination in the States works with a profound sense of alienation, so that it becomes directed solely towards the discovery of the artist's moral identity. Poetry in America may now have many social perquisites, but it is not yet a particularly social act. It is self-responsible and self-complete, and demands of the reader not so much his co-operation than his complete surrender. Like the American landscape, the poetry is often more impressive than that of England, but it is also considerably less intimate and, in a way, less vulnerable.

Perhaps it is their respect for the invulnerable

uniqueness of every poem that has made some of the American analytical critics so reluctant to pass judgments, despite the immense patience and love they lavish on their chosen works. They have often invigorating insights into the way a poem works, but they allow themselves very few as to what it may be worth. Hence both writers and critics in the States have a respect for technique that allows little room for the truth that even the most accomplished poets can be very dull indeed. Even Wallace Stevens, who is one of the greatest technical masters of our time, is in bulk impossible to read with sustained interest. And what is true of an important and original artist like Stevens is equally true of the innumerable academic craftsmen who aspire to Stevens's polish without the help of his imaginative drive.

Contemporary poetry in England, however, is no more exciting than that of America, and considerably less accomplished. Perhaps, on both sides of the Atlantic, we are going through a kind of psychological convalescence after the shocked, inarticulate poetry of the war. The work certainly has a wan, emptied-out air to it. Or perhaps the great outburst of originality which occurred in the 'twenties acts now more as a discouragement than a goad. Or perhaps, quite simply, we are in an interregnum; the real talent is not in poetry at the present.

I think there is some truth in each of these possible explanations. But there was also perhaps something radically wrong with the whole cult of "modernism". As an effort to make room in poetry for the full adult intelligence, with all its constantly varying and often conflicting emotions and its half-hidden, difficult motives, the "modern" movement can only have been a movement for health. But perhaps it set its standards of intelligence so high that only the absolutely first-rate artists could survive; whereas in fact poetry relies for its continuity and influence as much on its minor as its major figures. Certainly, the movement was never quite completed—or rather, the influence of many of the poets who did reach their full growth was oddly sterile. That is the burden of the epilogue to *New Bearings*. My own opinion is that if Eliot represented everything that was most important in modern poetry, he never had quite the influence in England that seemed his due because his essential preoccupations as a literary master were American; if he revalued the English tradition, it was only in the process of creating for himself a *cosmopolitan* tradition. In the chapter on Auden, I tried to show how modernism ran aground in this country after colliding with the merely contemporary. What happened in the States was answered by the way in a lecture R. P. Blackmur delivered recently at the Library of Congress in Washington:

> The two great internal facts of our time are the recreation of the devil (or pure behaviour) in a place of authority and the developments of techniques for finding destructive troubles in the psyche of individuals.

It is the last half of that sentence that makes me pause. The modern movement in poetry (and it comprises a number of movements: Imagism, Symbolism, Expressionism, and so on) began as an attempt by a number of original artists to find a medium which would express fully what they had to say. The subsequent

intense analysis of their work has reduced their discoveries to a series of techniques, "gimmicks", for
producing certain fashionable effects. The sense of
personal urgency which runs under all creative effort,
the urgency which makes the work of art take the form
it has to, often almost despite the artist, has been
reduced to a series of technical procedures which turn
out poetry as a mass-production line turns out cars.

Since there was in the States little or no usable
common ground for poetry, the insistence on technique
was necessary. Perhaps when the nagging concern with
fashionable language and method has quieted down it
will be found that the idiom of American poetry has in
fact, and without anyone quite realizing it, been staked
out. If so, the techniques will again join force with the
real American vitality. On the other hand, in England,
where the experimental element of modernism was more
grafted on than natural, the preoccupation with complexity has served best as a reminder of the standards
of intelligence expected in all good poetry and powerfully present elsewhere in the English tradition. In the
poetry of both countries what has been most important
is the effort to undercut conventional and worn-out
"poetic" material and means. The modern movement
has given the poet the chance to speak purely in terms
of his own artistic originality. It is the nature and effect
of this various originality which I have tried to illustrate
in this book.